Meet the

- Maltese are members of the Toy Group.

- Evidence of dogs resembling the Maltese has been found in ancient drawings, art and writings from as early as 5000–2000 B.C.

- The Maltese originated in Malta, an island near Italy in the Mediterranean Sea.

- The Maltese has lived a luxurious life as a favorite lapdog of fashionable men and women, being carried wherever his master went.

- The Maltese is distin- guished from all other breeds of dogs as the only dog with a long, silky, white coat.

- When it comes to grooming, the Maltese is a high-maintenance dog. His fine coat should be treated like human hair— brushed every day and washed and trimmed regularly.

- The Maltese is a very healthy breed. Generally, they live well into their teens and can be expected to be as playful and mischievous as when they were pups.

- Maltese are spirited, intelligent, sensitive and responsive dogs, which makes them easy to train.

Consulting Editor
IAN DUNBAR PH.D., MRCVS

Featuring Photographs by
JEANNIE AND BANE HARRISON

Howell Book House

An Imprint of Macmillan General Reference USA
A Pearson Education Macmillan Company
1633 Broadway
New York, NY 10019-6785

Macmillan Publishing books may be purchased for business or sales promotional use. For information please write: Special Markets Department, Macmillan Publishing USA, 1633 Broadway, New York, NY 10019.

Library of Congress Cataloging-in-Publication Data
The essential maltese / consulting editor, Ian Dunbar : featuring photographs by Jeanne & Bane Harrison.
         p.   cm.
Includes bibliographical references (p. 86) and index.
    ISBN 1-58245-084-6
    1. Maltese dog.   I. Title
SF429.M25D86   1999   98-55111
636.76—dc21   CIP

Manufactured in the United States of America
10 9 8 7 6 5 4 3 2 1

Series Director: Michele Matrisciani
Production Team: Angel Perez, Heather Pope, and
    Donna Wright
Book Design: Paul Costello
Photography: Jeannie and Bane Harrison

ARE YOU READY?!

☐ Have you prepared your home and your family for your new pet?

☐ Have you gotten the proper supplies you'll need to care for your dog?

☐ Have you found a veterinarian that you (and your dog) are comfortable with?

☐ Have you thought about how you want your dog to behave?

☐ Have you arranged your schedule to accommodate your dog's needs for exercise and attention?

No matter what stage you're at with your dog—still thinking about getting one, or he's already part of the family—this Essential guide will provide you with the practical information you need to understand and care for your canine companion. Of course you're ready—you have this book!

Maltese

CHAPTER ONE:

Getting to Know Your Maltese .1

CHAPTER TWO:

Homecoming 5

CHAPTER THREE:

To Good Health .15

CHAPTER FOUR:

Positively Nutritious 32

CHAPTER FIVE:

Putting on the Dog 39

CHAPTER SIX:

Measuring Up 52

CHAPTER SEVEN:

A Matter of Fact 58

CHAPTER EIGHT:

On Good Behavior .63

CHAPTER NINE:

Resources 86

Index 90

SIGHT

Maltese, like all dogs, can detect movement at a greater distance than we can, while they can't see as well up close. They can also see better in less light, but can't distinguish many colors.

SOUND

Maltese can hear about four times better than we can, and they can hear high-pitched sounds especially well.

TASTE

Maltese have fewer taste buds than we do, so they're likelier to try anything—and usually do, which is why it's important for their owners to monitor their food intake. Dogs are omnivorous, which means they eat meat as well as vegetables.

TOUCH

Maltese are social animals and love to be petted, groomed and played with.

SMELL

A Maltese's nose is his greatest sensory organ. A dog's sense of smell is so great he can follow a trail that's weeks old, detect odors diluted to one-millionth the concentration we'd need to notice them, even sniff out a person under water!

CHAPTER ONE

Getting to Know Your Maltese

Anyone who has become acquainted with a well-bred Maltese has a respect and affection for his attributes and his history. This spirited little breed is very intelligent, sensitive and responsive. Most of all, Maltese are extremely loving.

Your Maltese will constantly want to be your companion. He will be happy sitting by your side while you read a book or watch television. But he will also like to accompany you wherever you go. Maltese love to walk, day or night, winter, spring, summer or fall, even in the rain or snow. They make good watchdogs and will sound alarms when a

stranger comes to the door—but once the "stranger" is welcomed into the home, the Maltese will make friends with your guest. In fact, many fans of the breed have said that "they will kill you with their

Maltese love to be companions and want to accompany you wherever you go.

kisses" and "they would go home with strangers."

Maltese are one of several long-coated breeds, but they are the smallest and the only one with a pure white coat. The coat strongly resembles human hair, and people who may be allergic to other breeds of dogs or cats may find that they can get along just fine with a Maltese. They do not shed their coats seasonally like dogs with short coats, but because of their long hair they do require more maintenance than a shorthaired dog. Owners should expect to provide frequent grooming sessions or regular visits to a professional groomer.

A DELICATE BREED

Because of their delicate bone structure, Maltese can easily break bones falling off chairs, tables and when caught in the middle of a pile of overly zealous children. Maltese are definitely entertaining little characters, and with their love of people and their small size, many children are naturally drawn to them. If you have children that want a dog to roll and play with on the floor, you may wish to consider a different breed. In fact, many reputable Maltese breeders will not sell puppies to families with children under 6 or 7 years of age.

THE MALTESE AND OTHER PETS

Because of their lively personalities, Maltese usually get along well with most other animals in the household. But do remember that your Maltese will probably be the smallest dog in the home, and you may need to supervise a rambunctious larger dog closely when playing with a Maltese.

TAKE YOUR MALTESE WITH YOU

Maltese, as adoring little companions, love to travel with their owners. The easiest and safest way for your Maltese to travel with you is in his crate. If you will be going on a trip for an extended period of time, remember to take a few of your dog's favorite toys, his food and water dishes, a collar and leash and his food.

If you will be flying with your Maltese, he will need to visit his veterinarian to acquire a health certificate, ensuring his vaccinations are up-to-date and that he is healthy. A Maltese can travel in the cargo hold for a small charge, but traveling in

CHARACTER THE MA		
Elegant	Lively	Pl⋯
Loyal	Delicate	Intelligent
Friendly	Sensitive	

this area of the plane can be uncomfortable and frightening. Your dog will be much happier and safer traveling in a soft-sided specially designed pet carrier that most airlines allow in the passenger cabin. Make sure you check with your

The Maltese is the smallest of several long-coated breeds, but is the only breed with a pure white coat.

3

must
e their
altese with
care and children
must play gently
so as not to hurt
the delicate bone
structure of the
Maltese.

airline when making your travel plans and indicate that you will be traveling with your Maltese. While on the airplane in the passenger cabin, your Maltese should remain in his carrier. He will most likely spend most of the trip sleeping from the hum of the engines. Don't forget to take his traveling needs mentioned in the paragraph above.

CHAPTER TWO

Homecoming

The first weeks that your Maltese puppy is with you will be busy and demanding. There may be times when you wonder if getting a puppy was such a good idea. Things will go well if you have patience and keep your sense of humor. Remember that puppyhood only happens once. The extra effort you put into it now will pay off in the future.

PREPARING FOR YOUR PUPPY

Before you bring a new puppy into the house, there are some key items that you should have on hand.

Crates

Long ago, when dogs were still wild animals, they often slept in dens—shallow holes they dug in the ground, hidden away in places where they felt safe from predators. A "crate" is just a modern version of a den. Just as you enjoy having your own room where you can go for peace and privacy, your dog likes having her own room, too. As well as giving her a safe, cozy place to stay, crates can make training your dog a lot easier. Housebreaking goes much faster when you use a crate, and destructive chewing becomes easier to control. Traveling is safer for both you and your dog when she's in a crate.

The most popular crates are made of plastic or heavy welded steel wire. Plastic crates are lightweight, portable and are easily disassembled for storage or travel.

A crate need only be big enough for the dog to stand up, turn around and lie down comfortably. The crate should be large enough for your Maltese to stretch out on her side to sleep.

Bedding

When your puppy first comes home, she will need a lot of rest following her exuberant and playful excursions in her new environment. It is important to find a place for the puppy's bed that is out of the mainstream of the household traffic that will allow her to get the rest she needs. If you have purchased a crate for your puppy, the crate makes an excellent bed. The addition of a

Dogs enjoy the peace and privacy they find in their crates.

Find a quiet place in the house for your puppy to sleep.

washable, soft pad should make the crate a cozy bed that your puppy may prefer for years to come. Look for crate pads that are made of silky fabrics.

Lightweight leashes and collars are best for a Maltese.

Leash and Collar

Your Maltese will need a leash and collar. Leather and metal collars do not work well on Maltese due to the hair around their necks—a metal collar can catch in the coat and the leather ones can wear it down. A thin, nylon, one-piece collar seems to work best for this breed. Many of these have a ring at one end to which a leash can be clipped. Select

PUPPY ESSENTIALS

To prepare yourself and your family for your puppy's homecoming, and to be sure your pup has what she needs, you should obtain the following:

Food and Water Bowls: One for each. We recommend stainless steel or heavy crockery—something solid but easy to clean.

Bed and/or Crate Pad: Something soft, washable and big enough for your soon-to-be-adult dog.

Crate: Make housetraining easier and provide a safe, secure den for your dog with a crate—it only looks like a cage to you!

Toys: As much fun to buy as they are for your pup to play with. Don't overwhelm your puppy with too many toys, though, especially the first few days she's home. And be sure to include something hollow you can stuff with goodies, like a Kong.

I.D. Tag: Inscribed with your name and phone number.

Collar: An adjustable buckle collar is best. Remember, your pup's going to grow fast!

Leash: Style is nice, but durability and your comfort while holding it count, too.

Grooming Supplies: The proper brushes, special shampoo, toenail clippers, a toothbrush and doggy toothpaste.

a leash that is made from a similar, lightweight material. As an alternative, many Maltese owners prefer to use the loop-type, one-piece show leashes that have a slipknot closure. These leashes can be purchased from many of the catalog pet suppliers as well as at dog shows.

Water and Food Dishes

You will need small, lightweight bowls for food and water. These can be made from metal, plastic or a ceramic material. Many Maltese fanciers avoid using plastic bowls as there have been indications that they may be a cause of staining of the facial hair. Your breeder will let you know the food your puppy was eating, and it is wise to continue feeding the pup the same type of food, so as not to cause stomach upsets. If, over time, you want (or need) to change your dog's diet, do it by adding a little of the new food at a time. With their long coat, Maltese that drink water from water dishes get wet and sloppy faces. The wet facial hair can be a breeding ground for yeast, which in turn causes tear staining. Many Maltese owners will offer their pets water from a water bottle, such as those used for rabbits to alleviate this problem.

Toys and Chewies

Relatively small toys are best for a Maltese. Look for squeaky and interactive toys. Maltese seem to particularly like the fuzzy, plush, soft toys as well as the latex chewable ones. The latter are great for exercising gums, and puppies like to chew! Notably, Maltese seem to want to chew on paper as puppies, and one solution to this is to give them an

Stainless steel food and water dishes are most sanitary and easiest to clean.

Puppies like chewable toys— and you want to encourage your Maltese to chew on her toys, not on your shoes!

empty toilet paper roll to carry around. A "nutritious" toy many enjoy is a mini-carrot or a piece of vegetable. Maltese are very inquisitive little pups. It is wise to have a good supply of toys for your puppy or she is sure to find her own—and you never know what she will drag out of your closet.

PUPPY-PROOF YOUR HOME

Raising a puppy is a lot like raising small children—they get into everything. Some of what they get into can be hazardous to their health or to your possessions. You can make life safer for the puppy and your furniture by getting rid of hazards and temptations ahead of time.

To a puppy, the world is brand-new and fascinating. She is seeing it all for the very first time and absolutely everything must be thoroughly investigated. Puppies do most of their investigating with their mouths.

Preventing destructive and dangerous chewing is much easier than constantly trying to correct the puppy. Look around your home and think carefully about its contents. Check for objects that could, and

A baby gate is a great way to protect your Maltese from household hazards.

should, be put up out of the way of a curious puppy. To make immovable items such as furniture unappealing, a spray of Bitter Apple can be applied to the legs. You may also want to use a little Bitter Apple spray on the woodwork around your floors. If there are rooms your puppy should be restricted from entering until she is well-trained and more reliable, install a baby gate or keep the doors to those rooms closed.

Take a walk around your yard looking for potential hazards. If your yard is fenced, check the boundaries and gates for openings that could be potential escape routes. A Maltese puppy is very little and can work her way through a remarkably small hole in a fence. The grass is always greener on the other side of the fence—even to a puppy. If your yard is not fenced, make a resolution right now that your puppy will never be allowed to run off leash without close supervision. Keep her safe by keeping her on leash.

If you have a swimming pool or spa, exercise extreme caution with a Maltese. Curiosity, as well as the need for a drink, can lead a Maltese easily "over the brink." Your Maltese can quickly become waterlogged, particularly if her coat is long.

HOUSEHOLD DANGERS

Curious puppies and inquisitive dogs get into trouble not because they are bad, but simply because they want to investigate the world around them. It's our job to protect our dogs from harmful substances, like the following:

In the Garage

antifreeze

garden supplies, like snail and slug bait, pesticides, fertilizers, mouse and rat poisons

In the House

cleaners, especially pine oil

perfumes, colognes, aftershaves

medications, vitamins

office and craft supplies

electric cords

chicken or turkey bones

chocolate, onions

some house and garden plants, like ivy, oleander and poinsettia

CREATE A SPACE FOR YOUR NEW PET

Decide where you will put the puppy's crate, and have it set up and ready for her arrival. Where to keep the crate

IDENTIFY YOUR DOG

It is a terrible thing to think about, but your dog could somehow, someday, get lost or stolen. For safety's sake, every dog should wear a buckle collar with an identification tag. A tag is the first thing a stranger will look for on a lost dog. Inscribe the tag with your dog's name and your name and phone number.

There are two ways to permanently identify your dog. The first is a tattoo, placed on the inside of your dog's thigh. The tattoo should be your Social Security number or your dog's AKC registration number. The second is a microchip, a rice-sized pellet that is inserted under the dog's skin at the base of the neck, between the shoulder blades. When a scanner is passed over the dog, it will beep, notifying the person that the dog has a chip. The scanner will then show a code, identifying the dog.

will depend on what's most convenient for you as well as the puppy's response. Many puppies don't like to be isolated in one part of the house while their family is in another, but some puppies won't settle down in their crates if there's too much activity going on around them. You might have to experiment with different locations until you learn what works best for both you and the puppy.

VISIT YOUR VETERINARIAN

Make an appointment with your veterinarian to give the puppy a complete checkup within seventy-two hours of your purchase. If you do not have a veterinarian, ask the breeder or local kennel club for a recommendation. Although the puppy has most likely been health-checked by the breeder, an examination is additional security against health problems. Bring along your pup's vaccination history and arrange a schedule for completion of her initial series of vaccinations.

USE A SCHEDULE

Work out a schedule for you and the puppy. Housetraining is much easier when the puppy's meals, exercise and playtimes are on a regular schedule throughout the day. Plan your housetraining schedule and create a game plan before the puppy arrives. It is strongly advised that you bring your puppy home on a weekend (and if possible, take a week or two off), in order to devote extra time to settling in and house-training those first few days.

Feeding Your Puppy

Generally, puppies should be fed three times a day until they are 3 months old. They should then be fed two times a day for the rest of their lives. If you are feeding a dry kibble, you may wish to soak the kibble in water to soften this for younger puppies. By the time they are 3 to 4 months old, they should be eating the kibble dry or with a little canned food mixed in. Do not give your puppy fresh milk. If you have problems getting your puppy to eat, you may consider adding a little cottage cheese or some baby food

meats to her kibble. (See chapter four for a thorough discussion of feeding and nutrition.)

SOCIALIZING YOUR PUPPY

Exposure to new environments, situations, people and animals is all part of the socialization process. If your dog has had limited exposure to the outside world, start slowly, keeping in mind that it may be stressful for your dog. Gradually add distractions and new locations. Socialization is like any other part of training, building on small successes to make

13

It is important that your Maltese visit the veterinarian for a complete check-up as soon as you bring her home.

Socializing her with people and other animals is very important. This Maltese meets a Miniature Schnauzer for the first time.

the foundation strong. Reward your Maltese when she exhibits relaxed behavior by using treats, praise, petting or play. Ask friends if you can bring the dog along when you go for a visit. Make a list of all the places you can take your dog and start bringing her with you. (For an extensive discussion on how to train your dog, see chapter eight.)

CHAPTER THREE

To Good Health

FIRST THINGS FIRST

The Maltese is basically a very healthy breed with few medical problems. However, it is important that Maltese owners are aware of a few inherited disorders specific to the breed.

Portosystemic Shunt

Portosystemic shunt is a congenital problem that can be seen in some Maltese. During gestation, the placenta delivers blood with food and oxygen from the mother through the umbilical vein. In order to make this work, there is a shunt from the liver venous circulation to the arterial circulation. At birth, the pressure within the circulatory system changes as respiration occurs and this closes the shunt, which eventually disappears. If this reverse in circulation does not occur, the liver is deprived of a blood supply and does not develop properly after birth. Many puppies can live with the small functioning portion of the

The Maltese is basically a very sound breed with few health problems.

liver for some time but eventually have problems and usually die if the situation is uncorrected.

Most shunts cause recognizable clinical signs by the time a dog is a young adult. Signs of protosystemic shunts include poor weight gain, sensitivity to sedatives (especially diazepam), depression, head pressing (pushing the head against a solid object), seizures, weakness, salivation, vomiting, poor appetite, increased drinking and urinating, balance problems and frequent urinary tract disease or early onset of bladder stones. If the signs of problems increase dramatically after eating, this is a strong supportive sign of a portosystemic shunt.

This malady can be diagnosed by a veterinarian. If portosystemic shunt is found, a low protein diet, which decreases the amount of ammonia produced by the dog, will be recommended. In almost all cases, surgery is necessary. A Maltese owner faced with portosystemic shunt should see a board-certified veterinary surgeon to discuss the procedure at length.

Luxated Patella

Patellar luxation is a dislocation of the kneecap (patella). It may result from injury or congenital (present at birth) deformities.

Luxated patellas or "slipped stifles" are a common orthopedic problem in small dogs. Female dogs are 1.5 times more likely to be affected than males.

The crippling effects of patellar luxation are related to the severity and duration of the luxation. The milder forms, especially in small breeds, show little or no signs, and only minimal treatment is required. Severe cases cause more intense pain, with limping.

Treatment ranges from rest (decreasing your pet's activity for one to two weeks) to surgical reconstruction of the knee joint. Treatment is based upon the severity of signs and your pet's age, breed and weight (obesity complicates surgery and convalescence). Satisfactory results are usually obtained if the joint degeneration has not progressed too far. Once the condition is repaired, most affected Maltese will make a satisfactory recovery.

Collapsing Trachea

When the trachea collapses, air can no longer move freely through it. Then the animal breathes with difficulty and exhibits a honking cough.

Causes include trauma to the windpipe, nerve damage, inherited tracheal weakness, degeneration of cartilage and abnormal airflow in and out of the lungs. This condition is commonly found in small breeds of dogs, including Maltese, and closely resembles kennel cough.

If your Maltese has any of the symptoms of collapsing trachea, you should visit your veterinarian. He should perform a complete physical examination. X-rays are often necessary to confirm a diagnosis of tracheal collapse. Depending on the severity of the condition, treatment may include surgery and/or medical therapy. In mild cases, a change in lifestyle of your Maltese may be all that is necessary. Some cases of collapsing trachea cannot be cured, and treatment is directed at decreasing the severity and frequency of breathing difficulties.

White Dog Shaker Syndrome

Small white dogs such as Maltese can develop severe tremors for unexplained reasons. These dogs usually have bizarre eye movements that get much worse when excited or stressed. The usual treatment for this is to give diazepam to control the tremors and predisone to control the symptoms. Veterinarians do not yet know the cause of this syndrome.

17

THE IMPORTANCE OF PREVENTIVE CARE

There are many aspects of preventive care with which Maltese owners should be familiar: Vaccinations, regular vet visits and tooth care are just some. The advantage of preventive care is that it prevents problems.

The earlier that illness is detected in the Maltese, the easier it is for the veterinarian to treat the problem. Owners can help ensure their dogs' health by being on the lookout for medical problems. All this requires is an eye for detail and a willingness to observe. Pay close attention to your Maltese, how he looks, how he acts. What is normal behavior? How does his coat usually look? What are his eating and sleeping patterns? Subtle changes can indicate a problem. Keep close tabs on what is normal for your Maltese, and if anything out of the ordinary develops, call the veterinarian.

Spaying and Neutering

Spaying or neutering—surgically altering the Maltese so she or he cannot reproduce—should be at the top of every owner's "To Do" list. Why?

First, every day thousands of puppies are born in the United States as a result of uncontrolled

You can help your dog maintain good health by practicing the art of preventive care. Take good care of your Maltese today and he will be healthy tomorrow.

breeding. For every pet living in a happy home today, there are four pets on the street or in abusive homes suffering from starvation, exposure, neglect or mistreatment. In six years, a single female dog and her offspring can be the source of 67,000 new dogs.

A second reason to spay or neuter your Maltese is to create a healthier, more well-adjusted pet that, in most cases, will live longer than an intact animal. A spayed female is no longer susceptible to pyrometra (infection of the uterus), and is less prone to mammary cancers. The procedure eliminates the behavior that accompanies the female's heat cycle. A neutered male is less likely to develop prostate or anal cancer and is less apt to roam. Marking behavior is also reduced by altering.

When should your Maltese be spayed or neutered? Recommendations vary among vets, but 6 months of age is commonly suggested. Ask your vet what age is best for your Maltese.

Vaccinations

Another priority on a Maltese owner's list of preventive care is vaccinations. Vaccinations protect the

ADVANTAGES OF SPAY/NEUTER

The greatest advantage of spaying (for females) or neutering (for males) your dog is that you are guaranteed that your dog will not produce puppies. There are too many puppies already available for too few homes. There are other advantages as well.

Advantages of Spaying

No messy heats.

No "suitors" howling at your windows or waiting in your yard.

No risk of pyometra (disease of the uterus) and decreased incidences of mammary cancer.

Advantages of Neutering

Decreased incidences of fighting, but does not affect the dog's personality.

Decreased roaming in search of bitches in season.

Decreased incidences of many urogenital diseases.

dog against a host of infectious diseases, preventing an illness itself and the misery that accompanies it.

Vaccines should be a part of every young puppy's health care, since youngsters are so susceptible to disease. To remain effective, vaccinations must be kept current.

19

PREVENTIVE CARE PAYS

Using common sense, paying attention to your dog and working with your veterinarian, you can minimize health risks and problems. Use vet-recommended flea, tick and heartworm preventive medications; feed a nutritious diet appropriate for your dog's size, age and activity level; give your dog sufficient exercise and regular grooming; train and socialize your dog; keep current on your dog's shots; and enjoy all the years you have with your friend.

Good Nutrition

Dogs that receive the appropriate nutrients daily will be healthier and stronger than those that do not. The proper balance of proteins, fats, carbohydrates, vitamins, minerals and sufficient water enables the dog to remain healthy by fighting off illness.

Routine Checkups

Regular visits to the veterinary clinic should begin when your Maltese is a young pup and continue throughout his life. Make this a habit and it will certainly contribute to your Maltese's good health. Even if your Maltese seems perfectly healthy, a checkup once or twice a year is in order. Even if your dog seems fine to you, he could have an ongoing problem. Your veterinarian is trained to notice subtle changes or hints of illness.

Well-Being

Aside from the dog's physical needs—a proper and safe shelter, nutritious diet, health care and regular exercise—the Maltese needs plenty of plain, old-fashioned love. The dog is happiest when he is part of a family, enjoying the social interactions, nurturing and play. Bringing the Maltese into the family provides him with a sense of security.

COMMON DISEASES

Unfortunately, even with the best preventive care, the Maltese can fall ill. Infectious diseases, which are commonly spread from dog to dog via infected urine, feces or other body secretions, can wreak havoc. Following are a few of the diseases that can affect your pet.

Rabies

Probably one of the most well-known diseases that can affect dogs, rabies can strike any warm-blooded animal (including humans)—and is fatal. The rabies virus, which is present in an affected animal's saliva, is usually spread through a bite or open wound. The signs of the disease can be subtle at first. Normally friendly pets can become irritable and withdrawn. Shy pets may become overly friendly. Eventually, the dog becomes withdrawn and avoids light, which hurts the eyes of a rabid dog. Fever, vomiting and diarrhea are common.

Once these symptoms develop, the animal will die; there is no treatment or cure.

Since rabid animals may have a tendency to be aggressive and bite, animals suspected of having rabies should only be handled by animal control handlers or veterinarians.

Rabies is preventable with routine vaccines, and such vaccinations are required by law for domestic animals in all states in this country.

Parvovirus

Canine parvovirus is a highly contagious and devastating illness. The hardy virus is usually transmitted through contaminated feces, but it can be carried on an infected dog's feet or skin. It strikes dogs of all ages and is most serious in young puppies.

There are two main types of parvovirus. The first signs of the diarrhea-syndrome type are usually depression and lack of appetite, followed by vomiting and the characteristic bloody diarrhea. The dog appears to be in great pain, and he usually has a high fever.

The cardiac-syndrome type affects the heart muscle and is most common in young puppies. Puppies with this condition will stop

Maltese are happy just sitting by your side or in your lap.

21

YOUR PUPPY'S VACCINES

Vaccines are given to prevent your dog from getting infectious diseases like canine distemper or rabies. Vaccines are the ultimate preventive medicine: They're given before your dog ever gets the disease so as to protect him from the disease. That's why it is necessary for your dog to be vaccinated routinely. Puppy vaccines start at 8 weeks of age for the five-in-one DHLPP vaccine and are given every three to four weeks until the puppy is 16 months old. Your veterinarian will put your puppy on a proper schedule and will remind you when to bring in your dog for shots.

nursing, whine and gasp for air. Death may occur suddenly or in a few days. Youngsters that recover can have lingering heart failure that eventually takes their life.

Veterinarians can treat dogs with parvovirus, but the outcome varies. It depends on the age of the animal and severity of the disease. Treatment may include fluid therapy, medication to stop the severe diarrhea and antibiotics to prevent or stop secondary infection.

Young puppies receive some antibody protection against the disease from their mother, but they lose it quickly and must be vaccinated to prevent the disease. In most cases, vaccinated puppies are protected against the disease.

Coronavirus

Canine coronavirus is especially devastating to young puppies, causing depression, lack of appetite, vomiting that may contain blood and characteristically yellow-orange diarrhea. The virus is transmitted through feces, urine and saliva, and the onset of symptoms is usually rapid.

Dogs suffering from coronavirus are treated similarly to those suffering from parvovirus: fluid therapy, medication to stop diarrhea and vomiting and antibiotics if necessary.

Vaccinations are available to protect puppies and dogs against the virus and are recommended especially for those dogs in frequent contact with other dogs.

Distemper

Caused by a virus, distemper is highly contagious and is most common in unvaccinated puppies aged 3 to 8 months, but older dogs are susceptible as well. Fortunately, due to modern-day vaccines, distemper is no longer the killer it was fifty years ago.

It is especially important to vaccinate bitches before breeding to ensure maternal antibodies in the pups.

Hepatitis

Infectious canine hepatitis can affect dogs of every age, but it is most severe in puppies. It primarily affects the dog's liver, kidneys and lining of the blood vessels. Highly contagious, it is transmitted through urine, feces and saliva.

This disease has several forms. In the fatal fulminating form, the dog becomes ill very suddenly, develops bloody diarrhea and dies. In the acute form, the dog develops a fever, has bloody diarrhea, vomits blood and refuses to eat. Jaundice may be present; the whites of the dog's eyes appear yellow. Dogs with a mild case are lethargic or depressed and often refuse to eat.

Infectious canine hepatitis must be diagnosed and confirmed with a blood test. Ill dogs require hospitalization. Hepatitis is preventable in dogs by keeping vaccinations current.

23

Maintaining your Maltese's health means exercising them regularly.

Lyme Disease

Lyme disease has received a lot of press recently, with its increased incidence throughout the United States. The illness, caused by the bacteria *Borrelia burgdorferi,* is carried by ticks. It is passed along when the tick bites a victim, canine or human. (The dog cannot pass the disease to people, though. It is only transmitted via the tick.) It is most common during the tick season in May through August.

In dogs, the disease manifests itself in sudden lameness, caused by swollen joints, similar to arthritis. The dog is weak and may run a fever. The lameness can last a few days or several months, and some dogs have recurring difficulties.

Antibiotics are very effective in treating Lyme disease, and the sooner it is diagnosed and treated, the better. A vaccine is available; ask your veterinarian if your dog would benefit from it.

Kennel Cough

"Kennel cough," or the more politically correct "canine cough," shows itself as a harsh, dry cough. This contagious disease has been termed "kennel cough," much to the dismay of kennel owners, because of its often rapid spread through kennels. The cough may persist for weeks and is often followed by a bout of chronic bronchitis.

Many kennels require proof of bordatella vaccination before boarding. If your dog is in and out of kennels frequently, vaccination certainly is not a bad idea.

FIRST AID

First aid is not a substitute for professional care, though it can help save a dog's life.

To Stop Bleeding

Bleeding from a severe cut or wound must be stopped right away. There are two basic techniques—direct pressure and the tourniquet.

Try to control bleeding first by using direct pressure. Ask an assistant to hold the injured Maltese and place several pads of sterile gauze

Three types of ticks (l-r): the wood tick, brown dog tick and deer tick.

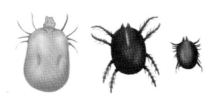

over the wound. Press. Do not wipe the wound or apply any cleansers or ointments. Apply firm, even pressure. If blood soaks through the pad, do not remove it as this could disrupt clotting. Simply place another pad on top and continue to apply pressure.

If bleeding on a leg or the tail does not stop by applying pressure, try using a tourniquet. Use this only as a last resort. A tourniquet that is left on too long can result in limb loss.

If the dog is bleeding from his mouth or anus, or vomits or defecates blood, he may be suffering from internal injuries. Do not attempt to stop bleeding. Call the veterinarian right away for emergency treatment.

Shock

Whenever a dog is injured or is seriously ill, the odds are good that he will go into a state of shock. A decreased supply of oxygen to the tissues usually results in unconsciousness; pale gums; weak, rapid pulse; and labored, rapid breathing. If not treated, a dog will die from shock. The conditions of the dog should continue to be

WHEN TO CALL THE VETERINARIAN

In any emergency situation, you should call your veterinarian immediately. Try to stay calm when you call, and give the vet or the assistant as much information as possible before you leave for the clinic. That way, the staff will be able to take immediate, specific action when you arrive. Emergencies include:

- Bleeding or deep wounds
- Hyperthermia (overheating)
- Shock
- Dehydration
- Abdominal Pain
- Burns
- Fits
- Unconsciousness
- Broken bones
- Paralysis

Call your veterinarian if you suspect any health troubles.

treated, but the dog should be as comfortable as possible. A blanket can help keep a dog warm. A dog in shock needs immediate veterinary care.

Maltese are curious and inquisitive; it is important to know the first-aid basics—just in case.

Regular veterinary checkups, daily exercise, balanced nutrition and a lot of old-fashioned TLC will help keep your Maltese happy and healthy.

Poisoning

A dog's curiosity will often lead him to eat or lick things he shouldn't. Unfortunately, many substances are poisonous to dogs, including household products, plants or chemicals. Owners must learn to act quickly if poisoning is suspected because the results can be deadly.

If your dog appears to be poisoned:

- Call your veterinarian and follow his or her directions.

- Try to identify the poison source—this is really important. Take the container or plant to the clinic.

Heatstroke

Heatstroke can be deadly and must be treated immediately to save the dog. Signs include rapid panting, darker-than-usual gums and tongue, salivating, exhaustion or vomiting. The dog's body temperature is elevated, sometimes as high as 106°F. If the dog is not treated, coma and death can follow.

If heatstroke is suspected, cool down your overheated dog as quickly as possible and call your veterinarian. Mildly affected dogs can be moved to a cooler environment, into an air-conditioned home, for example, or wrapped in moistened towels.

Insect Bites/Stings

Just like people, dogs can suffer bee stings and insect bites. Bees, wasps and yellow jackets leave a nasty, painful sting, and if your dog is stung repeatedly, shock can occur.

If an insect bite is suspected, try to identify the culprit. Remove the

POISON ALERT

If your dog has ingested a potentially poisonous substance, waste no time. Call the National Animal Poison Control Center hot line:

(800) 548-2423 ($30 per case) or

(900) 680-0000 ($20 first five minutes; $2.95 each additional minute)

stinger if it is a bee sting, and apply a mixture of baking soda and water to the sting. It is also a good idea to apply ice packs to reduce inflammation and ease pain. Call your veterinarian, especially if your dog seems ill or goes into shock.

INTERNAL PARASITES

Dogs are susceptible to several internal parasites. Keeping your Maltese free of internal parasites is another important aspect of health care.

Watch for general signs of poor condition: a dull coat, weight loss, lethargy, coughing, weakness and diarrhea.

For proper diagnosis and treatment of internal parasites, consult a veterinarian.

27

WHAT'S WRONG WITH MY DOG?

We've listed some common symptoms of health problems and their possible causes. If any of the following conditions appear serious immediately or persist for more than 24 hours, make an appointment to see your veterinarian immediately.

CONDITIONS	POSSIBLE CAUSES
DIARRHEA	Intestinal upset, typically caused by eating something bad or overeating. Can also be a viral infection, a bad case of nerves or anxiety or a parasite infection. If you see blood in the feces, get to the vet right away.
VOMITING/RETCHING	Dogs regurgitate fairly regularly (bitches for their young), whenever something upsets their stomach, or even out of excitement or anxiety. Often dogs eat grass, which, because it's indigestible in its pure form, irritates their stomachs and causes them to vomit. Getting a good look at *what* your dog vomited can better indicate what's causing it.
COUGHING	Obstruction in the throat; virus (kennel cough); roundworm infestation; congestive heart failure.
RUNNY NOSE	Because dogs don't catch colds like people, a runny nose is a sign of congestion or irritation.
LOSS OF APPETITE	Because most dogs are hearty and regular eaters, a loss of appetite can be your first and most accurate sign of a serious problem.
LOSS OF ENERGY (LETHARGY)	Any number of things could be slowing down your dog, from an infection to internal tumors to overexercise—even overeating.

ROUNDWORMS

Roundworms, or ascarids, are probably the most common worms that affect dogs. Most puppies are born with these organisms in their intestines, which is why youngsters are treated for these parasites as soon as it is safe to do so.

CONDITIONS	POSSIBLE CAUSES
STINKY BREATH	Imagine if you never brushed your teeth! Foul-smelling breath indicates plaque and tartar buildup that could possibly have caused infection. Start brushing your dog's teeth.
LIMPING	This could be caused by something as simple as a hurt or bruised pad, to something as complicated as hip dysplasia, torn ligaments or broken bones.
CONSTANT ITCHING	Probably due to fleas, mites or an allergic reaction to food or environment (your vet will need to help you determine what your dog's allergic to).
RED, INFLAMED, ITCHY SPOTS	Often referred to as "hot spots," these are particularly common on coated breeds. They're caused by a bacterial infection that gets aggravated as the dog licks and bites at the spot.
BALD SPOTS	These are the result of excessive itching or biting at the skin so that the hair follicles are damaged; excessively dry skin; mange; calluses; and even infections. You need to determine what the underlying cause is.
STINKY EARS/HEAD SHAKING	Take a look under your dog's ear flap. Do you see brown, waxy buildup? Clean the ears with something soft and a special cleaner, and don't use cotton swabs or go too deep into the ear canal.
UNUSUAL LUMPS	Could be fatty tissue, could be something serious (infection, trauma, tumor). Don't wait to find out.

29

Animals contract roundworms by ingesting infected soil and feces. A roundworm infestation can rob vital nutrients from young puppies and cause diarrhea, vomiting and digestive upset. Roundworms can also harm a young animal's liver and lungs, so treatment is imperative.

Tapeworms

Tapeworms are commonly transmitted by fleas to dogs. Tapeworm eggs enter the body of a canine host when the animal accidentally ingests a carrier flea. The parasite settles in the intestines, where it sinks its head into the intestinal wall and feeds off material the host is digesting. The worm grows a body of egg packets, which break off periodically and are expelled from the body in the feces. Fleas then ingest the eggs from the feces and the parasite's life cycle begins all over again.

External parasites, intense heat and insect bites and stings can threaten your Maltese.

Hookworms

Hookworms are so named because they hook onto an animal's small intestine and suck the host's blood. Like roundworms, hookworms are contracted when a dog ingests contaminated soil or feces.

Hookworms can be especially devastating to dogs. They will become thin and sick; puppies can die. An affected dog will suffer from bloody diarrhea and, if the parasites migrate to the lungs, the dog may contract bronchitis or pneumonia.

Hookworms commonly strike puppies 2 to 8 weeks of age and are less common in adult dogs.

Whipworms

Known for their thread-like appearance, whipworms attach into the wall of the large intestine to feed. Thick-shelled eggs are passed in the feces and in about two to four weeks are mature and able to reinfect a host that ingests the eggs.

Mild whipworm infestation is often without signs, but as the worms grow, weight loss, bloody diarrhea and anemia follow. In areas where the soil is heavily contaminated, frequent checks are advised to prevent severe infestation.

Heartworms

Heartworms larvae are transmitted by the ordinary mosquito, but the effects are far from ordinary. In three to four months, the larvae (microfilaria) become small worms and make their way to a vein, where they are transported to the heart, where they grow and reproduce.

At first, a dog with heartworms is free of symptoms. The signs vary, but the most common is a deep cough and shortness of breath. The dog tires easily, is weak and loses weight. Eventually, the dog may suffer from congestive heart failure.

EXTERNAL PARASITES

FLEAS—Besides carrying tapeworm larvae, fleas bite and suck the host's blood. Their bites itch and are extremely annoying to dogs, especially if the dog is hypersensitive to the bite. Fleas must be eliminated on the dog with special shampoos and dips. Fleas also infest the dog's bedding and the owner's home and yard.

TICKS—Several varieties of ticks attach themselves to dogs, where

FLEAS AND TICKS

There are so many safe, effective products available now to combat fleas and ticks that—thankfully—they are less of a problem. Prevention is key, however. Ask your veterinarian about starting your puppy on a flea/tick repellant right away. With this, regular grooming and environmental controls, your dog and your home should stay pest-free. Without this attention, you risk infesting your dog and your home, and you're in for an ugly and costly battle to clear up the problem.

31

they burrow into the skin and suck blood. Ticks can be carriers of several diseases, including Lyme disease and Rocky Mountain Spotted Fever.

LICE—Lice are not common in dogs, but when they are present they cause intense irritation and itching. There are two types: biting and sucking. Biting lice feed on skin scales, and sucking lice feed on blood.

MITES—There are several types of mites that cause several kinds of mange, including sarcoptic, demodectic and cheyletiella. These microscopic mites cause intense itching and misery to the dog.

CHAPTER FOUR

Positively Nutritious

The nutritional needs of a dog change throughout her lifetime. It is necessary to be aware of these changes not only for proper initial growth to occur, but also so your dog can lead a healthy life for many years.

Before bringing your puppy home, ask the breeder for the puppy's feeding schedule and information about what and how much she is used to eating. Maintain this regimen for at least the first few days before gradually changing to a schedule that is more in line with your family's lifestyle. The breeder may supply you with a small quantity of the food the puppy has been eating. Use this or have your own supply of the same food ready when you bring your puppy home.

After the puppy has been with you for three days and has become acclimated to her new environment, you can begin a gradual food change. Add more new food to the usual food each day until it has entirely replaced the previous diet.

LIFE-STAGE FEEDING

Puppies and adolescent dogs require a much higher intake of protein, calories and nutrients than adult dogs due to the demands of their rapidly developing bodies. Most commercial brands of dry kibble meet these requirements and are well balanced for proper growth. The majority of puppy foods now available are so carefully planned that it is unwise to add anything other than water to them.

The major ingredients of most dry dog foods are chicken, beef or lamb by-products; and corn, wheat or rice. The higher the meat content, the higher the protein percentage, palatability and digestibility of the food. Protein percentages in puppy food are usually between 25 and 30 percent. There are many advantages of dry foods over semimoist and canned dog foods for

GROWTH STAGE FOODS

Once upon a time, there was puppy food and there was adult dog food. Now there are foods for puppies, young adults/active dogs, less active dogs and senior citizens. What's the difference between these foods? They vary by the amounts of nutrients they provide for the dog's growth stage/activity level.

Less active dogs don't need as much protein or fat as growing, active dogs; senior dogs don't need some of the nutrients vital to puppies. By feeding a high-quality food that's appropriate for your dog's age and activity level, you're benefiting your dog and yourself. Feed too much protein to a couch potato and she'll have energy to spare, which means a few more trips around the block will be needed to burn it off. Feed an adult diet to a puppy, and risk growth and development abnormalities that could affect her for a lifetime.

33

A well-fed puppy has bright eyes, a shiny coat and lots of energy.

How to Read the Dog Food Label

With so many choices on the market, how can you be sure you are feeding the right food to your dog? The information is all there on the label—if you know what you're looking for.

Look for the nutritional claim right up top. Is the food "100 percent nutritionally complete"? If so, it's for nearly all life stages; "growth and maintenance," on the other hand, is for early development; puppy foods are marked as such, as are foods for senior dogs.

Ingredients are listed in descending order by weight. The first three or four ingredients will tell you the bulk of what the food contains. Look for the highest-quality ingredients, like meats and grains, to be among them.

The Guaranteed Analysis tells you what levels of protein, fat, fiber and moisture are in the food, in that order. While these numbers are meaningful, they won't tell you much about the quality of the food. Nutritional value is in the dry matter, not the moisture content.

In many ways, seeing is believing. If your dog has bright eyes, a shiny coat, a good appetite and a good energy level, chances are her diet's fine. Your dog's breeder and your veterinarian are good sources of advice if you're still confused.

puppies and normal, healthy adult Maltese.

It is best to feed meals that are primarily dry food because the chewing action involved in eating a dry food is better for teeth and gum health. Dry food is also less expensive than canned food of equal quality.

Dogs whose diets are based on canned or soft foods have a greater likelihood of developing calcium deposits and gum disease. Canned or semimoist foods do serve certain functions, however. As a supplement to dry dog food, in small portions, canned or semimoist foods can be useful to stimulate appetites and aid in weight gain. But unless very special conditions exist, they are not the best way for a dog to meet her food needs.

A Feeding Schedule

By the time you bring your puppy home, she will probably be at the stage where three meals will suffice. Your new puppy should be fed morning, midday and evening. Fresh water should be available to her at all times. A good plan to follow is to divide the amount recommended by the veterinarian by three. If the

Your Maltese's nutritional requirements will change throughout her lifetime.

puppy is finishing all three of these portions throughout the day and the appearance of the body indicates proper growth, then stay with those amounts. If the puppy looks like she is gaining weight excessively, then reduce the amount that is given. The same applies for the puppy that leaves quantities of food uneaten, yet is at a good weight and energy level otherwise. Obviously, if a puppy is eating her rations and appears thin, her food intake should be increased. This is something that can only be accomplished by observation and good judgment.

Puppies and adolescent dogs require a high intake of nutrients to fuel their rapidly developing bodies.

FOOD ALLERGIES

If your puppy or dog seems to itch all the time for no apparent reason, she could be allergic to one or more ingredients in her food. This is not uncommon, and it's why many foods contain lamb and rice instead of beef, wheat or soy. Have your dog tested by your veterinarian, and be patient while you strive to identify and eliminate the allergens from your dog's food (or environment).

From 6 months to 1 year of age, the puppy should remain on puppy food, but the feedings should decrease to twice a day. By the time a dog reaches 1 year of age, she should be switched to an adult maintenance diet. The number of feedings can remain at twice a day, though it is easier for most owners to feed a large meal once a day.

Puppies and dogs should have a place of their own where they can eat their meals without disturbance. A dog's crate can be an ideal place to feed a dog. Give the dog a definite period of time to eat her food rather than allowing her to nibble throughout the day. If the food has not been eaten within a ten-minute period, pick it up and do not feed again until the next mealtime. One of the best ways to spot health problems in dogs is monitoring their food intake.

Some owners like to add variety to their dogs' lives with human food. Scraps given regularly can lead to weight gain if the amount of the dog's regular food is not reduced. The risk of destroying the nutritional balance of the dog food also exists. Some human foods fed in large quantities can lead to gastrointestinal problems, which can result in loose stools and even diarrhea.

The amount of food an adult Maltese should eat daily will vary according to the size of the dog, her activity level and how much time she spends outside.

Most Maltese owners should consider placing their dog on a food that is very low in fat and protein content by the age of 8 or 9, unless the dog is still very active. A dog that is inactive either by choice or the owner's laziness has lower nutritional requirements. Another thing to keep in mind is that as dogs age, their kidneys can be destroyed if kept on a food with high protein content. Foods formulated for older dogs are low in fat and protein content.

Feeding your Maltese dry food helps keep her teeth and gums healthy.

Maintaining the proper weight and nutrition of an older Maltese is probably more difficult than weight maintenance at any other stage of the Maltese's life. A certain amount of body fat is necessary to protect her in the event of illness. Too much excess weight will make the dog even less active and more prone to physical problems. If a dog develops problems, such as kidney failure, heart disease or an overly sensitive digestive tract, specially formulated foods that are commercially available might be necessary.

The physical appearance a Maltese presents is as much a result of genetics as it is the food she eats. The owner that feeds a high-quality food and keeps her in optimum weight for her size will be rewarded with a Maltese whose health and fitness mirrors her diet.

HOW MANY MEALS A DAY

Individual dogs vary in how much they should eat to maintain a desired body weight—not too fat, but not too thin. Puppies need several meals a day, while older dogs may need only one. Determine how much food keeps your adult dog

One of the best ways to spot health problems in dogs is to monitor their food intake.

A great way to add variety to your Maltese's diet is to give her treats.

looking and feeling her best. Then decide how many meals you want to feed with that amount. Like us, most dogs love to eat, and offering two meals a day is more enjoyable for them. If you're worried about overfeeding, make sure you measure correctly and abstain from adding tidbits to the meals.

Whether you feed one or two meals, only leave your dog's food out for the amount of time it takes her to eat it—ten minutes, for example. Free-feeding (when food is available any time) and leisurely meals encourage picky eating. Don't worry if your dog doesn't finish all her dinner in the allotted time. She'll learn she should.

Putting on the Dog

Many Maltese owners ask what they need to do to have a beautiful coat on their Maltese. The answer is that good coats are "bred, fed and cared for." The most important part of keeping a beautiful coat is the grooming care your Maltese receives.

BASIC GROOMING SUPPLIES

You will need a pin brush, comb(s), slicker brush, scissors, nail clippers, rubber bands and hair dryer. When selecting a pin brush, choose one that has good deep pins; these are

GROOMING TOOLS

pin brush	scissors
slicker brush	nail clippers
flea comb	tooth-cleaning equipment
towel	shampoo
mat rake	conditioner
grooming glove	clippers

needed to penetrate the Maltese coat. The most basic comb is the Belgium Greyhound comb; these combs are made of steel and glide through the hair much better and break less coat than other kinds. Greyhound combs in both a large and small size are good to have in your grooming supplies. A rattail parting comb from the beauty supply store is another useful comb for making the straight part down the middle of the back. A small soft slicker brush is a must, and the triangle-shaped ones are particularly good for getting those difficult places like the underarms.

There are several varieties of nail clippers, but the preferred type for Maltese nails is the guillotine type. A good quality scissors is also needed to cut hair on the feet and around the face. The small orthodontic type of rubber bands or small barrettes are useful for holding the hair out of the face of the Maltese. A hair dryer is needed to dry the coat of your Maltese following his bath.

TRAINING TO BE GROOMED

Train your puppy to lay on his back and/or side and be groomed when he is young. The best time to train is when he is tired and willing to lie quietly or rest.

BRUSHING TECHNIQUES

Brushing your dog is the single most important thing that you can do to keep the coat looking nice and mat free. You must brush at least every other day if you have your dog in full coat. When brushing, continually mist the hair with a conditioner spray (for example, the conditioner used as a rinse after bathing). A tiny bit of coat oil may be added to the conditioner. The conditioning mist helps avoid breaking the coat.

It is important to brush the entire coat and not just the top portions. Start with a pin brush and work your way though the coat. Use the parting comb to separate the hair. Start at the underside and work up to the rest of the coat. The method that you use is important. A common problem many people have trying to grow a long coat is "flipping the wrists." The grooming stroke should be a long stroke through the hair finished off with the wrist flat. When one finishes the stroke by flipping up the wrist, microscopic pieces of hair can break off the ends of the coat. Over time, this repeated practice can cause a coat to discontinue growing.

Because your Maltese's hair is one of his best attributes, it is important to brush the coat frequently.

41

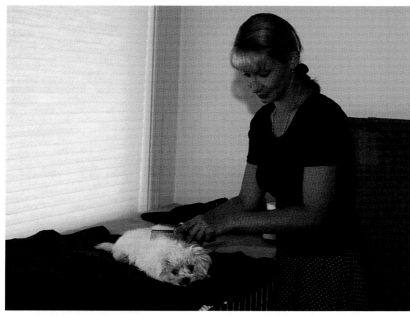

This pup was taught to lay quietly while being groomed.

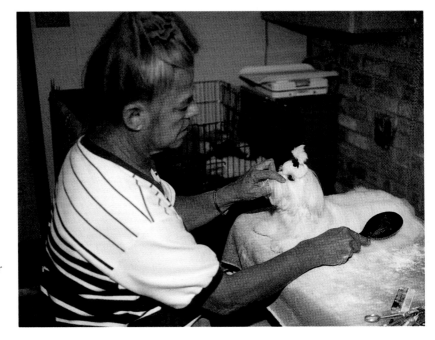

The grooming stroke should be a long stroke through the hair finished off with the wrist flat.

Parting

Stack your Maltese on a table and stand directly behind him. (Make sure the dog is standing so that his spine is straight.) Using the end tooth of a metal comb or a knitting needle and beginning at the base of the dog's neck, run the tooth of the comb straight down the spine, allowing the coat to fall to either side.

Removing Mats

If you find a mat, gently separate it with your fingertips. Brushing through it will result in hair loss. To remove a mat, spray it lightly with water to lubricate the hair. If the mat you are removing is large and packed solid, you may have to spray it with detangler or, better yet, a coat conditioning oil until it is saturated. You and your Maltese will both need a lot of patience. Pull the mat apart as much as possible with your fingers; then use the end tooth of the comb to loosen the individual hairs. Work on the mat from whichever side allows you the best access. Do not cut the mat out unless you want a big hole in your dog's coat, and only cut through the mat as a last resort, if it is so solidly packed that you have no other choice.

To loosen the mat, you may have to use more oil or detangler as you progress, and you may have to allow it to soak for a while before it does its job. Alternate between separating the mat with your fingers and separating it with the end tooth of your comb. Never try to pull the entire mat out at once with the comb or brush. It hurts your dog and he will let you know that he does not appreciate what you are doing.

The coat should be free of all mats before you bathe your Maltese; water only serves to set mats in tighter.

BATHING

A good bathing schedule for a Maltese would be to bathe every seven to ten days. Follow the shampoo with a conditioner. Care should be used during the shampoo process. Excessive rubbing can cause breakage and matting. The best results will be achieved by pouring the shampoo and conditioner over the coat and gently cleansing.

Have everything necessary at hand—towels, shampoo and conditioner—ready before you put your

43

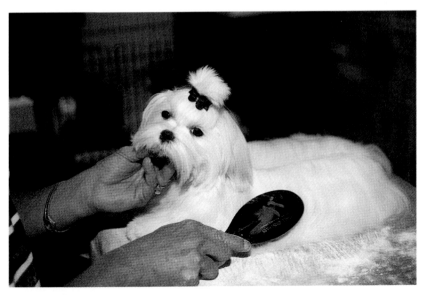

Brush hair to the side after parting it down the middle.

Rinse every part of the body until all traces of soap are gone.

44

Maltese in the tub. Clean your dog's ears if necessary and place a small ball of cotton in the ears to soak up any water accidentally entering the ear canal (a common cause of infection). Place a rubber mat or towel on the bottom of the sink or bathtub. A hand-held rubber spray attached to your faucet can make things much easier.

Make sure your Maltese is completely wet to the skin before applying shampoo. Apply dabs of shampoo to the back, each leg and under the tail of your dog. Work up a good lather down to the skin, proceeding from back to front. Take special care to clean the anal area and

paw pads. Rinse the coat thoroughly and shampoo again. Rinse again. Wash your dog's face with a washcloth. Take great care to avoid getting shampoo in the eyes. Tip the head up to rinse. Rinse every part of the body until all traces of soap are gone and the water runs perfectly clear.

At this point, you may add a conditioner. Allow it to stay in the coat for the time recommended by the manufacturer and then rinse from the coat. When the bath is finished, squeeze all the excess water from the ears, legs and tail before removing the dog from the tub. When towel drying your Maltese, squeeze or blot the coat with the towel to remove as much moisture as possible. Do not rub the coat with the towel as this can cause tangling and mats.

Which Shampoos to Use?

Using products designed for humans, which are acidic, will sooner or later cause damage to your Maltese's coat. There are a number of good canine products on the market. Select a shampoo that will cleanse well. Whitening shampoos may help brighten the coat of a Maltese, but long-term use of these products may cause dryness of the hair and result in coat breakage. Follow the shampoo with a good cream rinse or conditioner.

Blow Drying

Following the bath, a Maltese should be blown dry. Inexpensive stand dryers are available that work well for many people. This type of dryer will sit on a table or counter and allow the use of one hand to brush the Maltese hair and the other hand to keep your Maltese out of danger. Use only the medium heat setting of your dryer. Using high heat can cause the coat to break more readily. As you direct the heat from the dryer to the coat use a long, firm grooming stroke. Continue with one section until it feels dry to the touch and then move on to another. Many times the feet and leg furnishings can be dried easier using a slicker brush. The face furnishings should be dried last using a small metallic comb.

GROOMING FEET

The hair between the pads of the Maltese foot grows quite long and quite fast. If ignored, it tends to mat. Left alone, the mats increase in size and can spread the pads farther apart.

Keeping the pads neatly trimmed is an easy task. With the dog on his side or back, hold a leg steady at an angle that is comfortable for you. The hand that holds the leg will have to do double duty because you'll need to spread the pads slightly apart to trim down between them. Some groomers use a clipper (such as a mustache trimmer) for this task, others use small scissors.

Shaggy feet make even the most neatly groomed Maltese look "unfinished." The unkempt appearance of those feet can be improved simply by trimming and rounding the coat around the feet. Push the hair up and away from the foot itself and hold it there. Brush or comb a layer of hair over the foot and trim it all the way around fairly close to the foot. Then brush a second layer over the foot, this time trimming it so that it's slightly longer than the first layer. Depending on how heavily coated your dog's foot is, repeat this until the foot has a neat, rounded appearance. Do all four feet in the same way.

Nails should be clipped on a weekly basis— right after a bath, when the nails are soft, is a good time for a trim.

Trimming Nails

Clip your Maltese's nails under good lighting. Most Maltese nails are white or light colored, and the darker center of the quick is unmistakable. However, some Maltese have dark nails and the quick is not visible. In this case, clip only the ends of the nails. You may have to cut them more frequently to achieve a proper length. Cut at a perpendicular (90°) angle to the nail. Remember to also clip the nail of the dewclaws. After you clip them, filing the nails with a human or dog nail file helps to smooth the sharp edges.

CLEANING TEETH

Dogs should have their teeth brushed—every day if possible. This is especially important for older dogs that are more likely to have plaque buildup. Be sure to use toothpaste made for dogs. Toothpaste for humans contains ingredients that can upset a dog's stomach.

GROOMING EARS

Apply ear powder to the inside of each ear, making certain the hair is thoroughly covered, especially at the

QUICK AND PAINLESS NAIL CLIPPING

This is possible if you make a habit out of handling your dog's feet and giving your dog treats when you do. When it's time to clip nails, go through the same routine, but take your clippers and snip off just the ends of the nail—clip too far down and you'll cut into the "quick," the nerve center, hurting your dog and causing the nail to bleed. Clip two nails a session while you're getting your dog used to the procedure, and you'll soon be doing all four feet quickly and easily.

base. Wait a few minutes to allow the powder to dry the hair. It is surprising how much easier the hair is to pluck once the powder has dried and how much less your Maltese will mind the plucking if the powder is used.

Pluck only a few hairs at a time, because this is less irritating for the dog. You can use your fingers to pull out the majority of the hair; however, if you prefer, you may also use tweezers or a hemostat.

TEAR STAINING

There are several ways to remove tear staining from the facial hair.

Take care not to allow these products, or any other chemical solutions, to get in your dog's eyes. It is also important to remember that when attempting to remove tear staining you may also be damaging the hair; make sure that you condition the hair before you start. Pack the facial furnishings with a good quality conditioner for several days before removing the tear staining.

Mix an equal volume of milk of magnesia and human hair peroxide (20 volume), and then use cornstarch to make a good paste. Apply and work well into the stained area and let dry overnight. Wash out and condition well. Keep

47

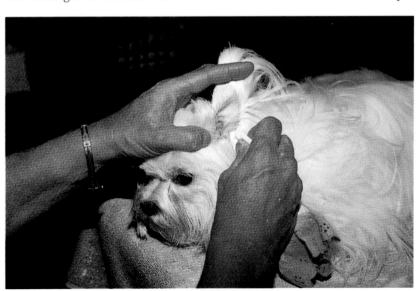

It is important to incorporate ear cleaning into your dog's grooming routine.

doing this for several days until tear staining is gone, skipping a day or two between applications if possible. Do not be impatient. If you have a face that is badly stained, it may take several attempts to bring the color back to white.

YELLOW STAINS

It is not unusual for Maltese to stain yellow on their feet from urine, mud and other things. A good formula to remove this yellow color is one made of 50 percent liquid Woolite and 50 percent human hair peroxide (20 volume), diluted with equal parts of water. Shampoo this mixture into the stained portion of the coat and let it remain for three to five minutes. Wash out and shampoo and condition as normal.

LEISURE TRIMS FOR ADULT MALTESE

Maintaining a long, flowing coat is a lot of work. The solution is a short trim known variously as a "leisure clip," "puppy cut," "cocker clip," "Poodle clip" or "Schnauzer cut."

Whatever you wish to call it, a short trim gives a Maltese freedom to play and be mischievous without the worry of coat care problems.

The directions that follow are for the Oster A5 clipper, using a #10 blade and a #4 or #5 blade. Oster clippers can be purchased from many of the catalog pet suppliers and many pet stores. There are other comparable brands of clippers.

Leisure Cut Procedure

First, groom your Maltese with a pin brush, slicker and comb until all the mats have been removed from the coat. Using the Oster clipper with the #4 or #5 blade, clip the hair of the body in a downward motion for a smooth finish. Clip all of the body from the neck to the tail, including the lower chest. Do not clip the legs, tail or head. An alternative is to leave the hair on the sides and the lower chest a little longer than the clipped body coat.

When you have finished clipping the body, you can use your scissors to trim the legs so that the hair blends into that of the body, leaving the hair longer toward the feet but shorter at the top. Round off the feet to give a nice finished look. Do not forget to trim the hair around the pads and clip the toenails.

Next, you should work on the head and face. Using the Oster clipper with the #10 blade, clip the hair on the sides of the face going from the front to the back. Clip the area under the ears short also. Leave the hair on the ears long. For the mustache and beard, use your scissors and trim the area from the corner of the mouth forward into a circle. The hair above the eyes and the skull should be trimmed to about 1 to 2 inches in length so it looks as though the dog is wearing a little cap. Hold the hair up to cut this in a nice circle and then let it fall. As you work on the face, you may wish to initially leave the hair a little longer—with practice, you will be able to cut so that you achieve the look you desire.

Once you have completed the clipping and scissoring you should bathe and blow-dry your Maltese. You may find you have missed a few straggly hairs, so touch them up with your scissors.

Once in this clip, your Maltese will need to only be clipped or touched up every several months.

Short trims, like this one, cut down on grooming and bathing time.

49

MAKING THOSE TOPKNOTS

The first step in making Maltese topknots is to use a little clear gel (human hair type) in the topknot area when drying the hair to give it a bit more body. To make topknots, you will need end papers, used for giving permanents to human hair, or mesh, some small orthodontic rubber bands and bows. The permanent end papers or mesh should be cut into squares approximately 2 inches by 2 inches.

Have your Maltese lay his head on a small pillow while making the

This owner gathers up hair for a single top-knot.

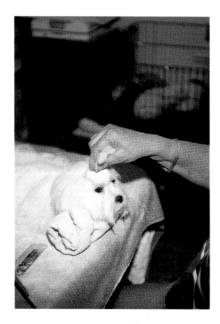

50

Next, secure the section with a small rubber band and apply a ribbon or bow for the finishing touch.

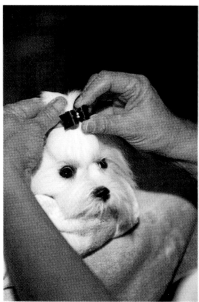

topknots. The pillow elevates the head and provides you with a good perspective so that you will not make the topknots too far back.

Start by using a rattail comb to part the hair straight back about the outside edge of each eye (approximately 1 inch above the eye). Make a part in the center and divide into two equal sections. Next, gather up the hair in each section. You may wish to back comb the section to give the hair a little more lift. Secure the section with a small rubber band. Use the rattail end of the comb to pull out any additional lift you desire in the front.

Next, take the end paper and fold over the top about one third. Place the fold on the top and wrap this around the rubber-banded portion of hair. Place the end paper in the back and fold each side over to the front and then wrap around to the back—folded in thirds.

Place the tail of the rattail comb behind the hair and end paper and fold the top portion over the rattail to give the resultant topknot a nice, even fold. Then use another small rubber band to secure the topknot.

Finish the topknots by using some gel to hold down any wispy

When it comes to grooming, Maltese can be high maintenance.

pieces of hair that are not secure in the topknot.

Finally, its time to apply the bows. Bows can be purchased from several suppliers, or you can make your own from satin ribbon. Small pieces of colored yarn also make attractive bows. Most owners prefer bows in red, royal blue, purple, green or black.

Maltese in the United States are shown with two topknots as adults. Many puppies are shown with single topknots because they may not have enough hair to make the two topknots. In Europe and Australia, Maltese are shown with a single topknot.

Single topknots are made by gathering the hair from just above the corner of each eye and, using a rattail comb, parting for about an inch toward the back of the dog's head. The resulting hank of hair is secured with a small rubber band. The rattail comb can be used in the front to get some additional lift if desired. Placing a large bow over the rubber band finishes the topknot.

CHOOSING A GROOMER

Because of the relatively elaborate techniques required to properly groom a Maltese, finding a good groomer may be a challenge. Ask your breeder and/or your veterinarian for references.

CHAPTER SIX

Measuring Up

Known and admired for thousands of years, the lovely Maltese with their silky white coats have always symbolized elegance and beauty wherever they go.

WHAT IS A BREED STANDARD?

All dogs come with four legs, a tail and a head with ears, eyes and a nose. So how do we differentiate a Maltese from other dogs? We use something called a standard. This blueprint is a description in simple words that depict the breed characteristics of a Maltese. It should, however, be remembered that the standard describes the "perfect" Maltese. But no dog is ever perfect, and no Maltese will possess every quality in the standard.

OFFICIAL STANDARD FOR THE MALTESE

GENERAL APPEARANCE—*The Maltese is a toy dog covered from head to foot with a mantle of long, silky, white hair. He is gentle-mannered and affectionate, eager and sprightly in action, and despite his size, possessed of the vigor needed for the satisfactory companion.*

The standard is very specific in specifying a "silky" coat. The coat should have the feel of a finely textured silk fabric, somewhat "cool" to the touch. The Maltese should be gentle in manner but still lively and vigorous. The Maltese is a devoted companion to her master but at the same time should not be shy of strangers.

HEAD—*Of medium length and in proportion to the size of the dog. The skull is slightly rounded on top, the stop moderate. The drop ears are rather low set and heavily feathered with long hair that hangs close to the head. Eyes are set not too far apart; they are very dark and round, their black rims enhancing the gentle yet alert expression. The muzzle is of medium length, fine and tapered but not snipy. The nose is black. The teeth meet in an even, edge-to-edge bit, or in a scissors bite.*

The shape of the head and the features of the Maltese impart the adorable look that has attracted so many to the breed. The overall balance of the head must be kept in perspective to the standard.

Many Maltese fans use the term "halos" when describing a Maltese head. While the standard makes no mention of halos, they are a characteristic that may enhance the overall appearance of the head. Halos are defined as the darkening of the skin around the eyes. Many times the presence of halos may be connected with good pigmentation, but there

The coat of a Maltese is described as silky and should have the feel of finely textured silk.

WHAT IS A BREED STANDARD?

A breed standard—a detailed description of an individual breed—is meant to portray the ideal specimen of that breed. This includes ideal structure, temperament, gait, type—all aspects of the dog. Because the standard describes an ideal specimen, it isn't based on any particular dog. It is a concept against which judges compare actual dogs and breeders strive to produce dogs. At a dog show, the dog that wins is the one that comes closest, in the judge's opinion, to the standard for its breed. Breed standards are written by the breed parent clubs, the national organizations formed to oversee the well-being of the breed. They are voted on and approved by the members of the parent clubs.

"Halos" are defined as a darkening of the skin around the eyes.

have been many outstanding specimens of the breed that do not have extensive halos.

NECK—*Sufficient length of neck is desirable as promoting a high carriage of the head.*

The high neck carriage gives the Maltese the elegance that distinguishes her from other breeds of dogs. It should also be noted that to have the proper high neck carriage, the Maltese should possess proper layback of the shoulders and construction of the front legs.

BODY—*Compact, the height from the withers to the ground equaling the length from the withers to the root of the tail. Shoulder blades are sloping, the elbows well knit and held close to the body. The back is level in topline, the ribs well sprung. The chest is fairly deep, the loins taut, strong, and just slightly tucked up underneath.*

The appearance of the Maltese should be of a compact or "cobby" dog. She should be square from the point of the withers to the base of the tail and from the point of the withers to the ground. The ideal angle of the shoulders should be 45°. Incorrect toplines will cause a

Maltese's back to have a rounded appearance or to be high in the hind quarters. Any tendency toward flatness in the ribs is also incorrect.

TAIL—*A long-haired plume carried gracefully over the back, its tip lying to the side over the quarter.*

The tail should be set high. A common fault with many Maltese is a low-set tail that causes the dog to look longer than it should and destroys the compact appearance. A tail with a feathered appearance or that is carried above the horizontal is also a serious fault.

LEGS AND FEET—*Legs are fine-boned and nicely feathered. Forelegs are straight, their pastern joints well knit and devoid of appreciable bend. Hind legs are strong and moderately angulated at stifles and hocks. The feet are small and round, with toe pads black. Scraggly hairs on the feet may be trimmed to give a neater appearance.*

The Maltese is one of only three toy breeds to mention fine bone in the standard, so it is important that this characteristic be present. The Maltese is a fine, delicate dog that originally was a "sleeve-dog" of the aristocracy. To maintain this position

THE AMERICAN KENNEL CLUB

Familiarly referred to as "the AKC," the American Kennel Club is a nonprofit organization devoted to the advancement of purebred dogs. The AKC maintains a registry of recognized breeds and adopts and enforces rules for dog events including shows, obedience trials, field trials, hunting tests, lure coursing, herding, earthdog trials, agility and the Canine Good Citizen program. It is a club of clubs, established in 1884 and composed, today, of over 500 autonomous dog clubs throughout the United States. Each club is represented by a delegate; the delegates make up the legislative body of the AKC, voting on rules and electing directors. The American Kennel Club maintains the Stud Book, the record of every dog ever registered with the AKC, and publishes a variety of materials on purebred dogs, including a monthly magazine, books and numerous educational pamphlets. For more information, contact the AKC at the address listed in Chapter 9, "Resources."

55

in the early times, it was important that they retain this fineness. Any suggestion of large bones and a larger size is still a serious fault.

COAT AND COLOR—*The coat is single, that is, without undercoat. It hangs long, flat, and silky over the sides*

The Maltese coat is long, flat and silky.

of the body almost, if not quite, to the ground. The long head-hair may be tied up in a topknot or it may be left hanging. Any suggestion of kinkiness, curliness, or woolly texture is objectionable. Color, pure white. Light tan or lemon on the ears is permissible, but not desirable.

A true "silky" coat is one that falls flat to the body.

SIZE—*Weight under 7 pounds, with 4 to 6 pounds preferred. Over-all quality is to be favored over size.*

The standard is very clear on the issue of size. Maltese are toy dogs and the size must be maintained in

The Maltese is a toy dog and should weigh between 4 and 6 pounds.

this range to meet the overall balance and elegant appearance of the breed.

GAIT—*The Maltese moves with a jaunty, smooth, flowing gait. Viewed from the side, he gives an impression of rapid movement, size considered. In the stride, the forelegs reach straight and free from the shoulders, with elbows close. Hind legs to move in a straight line. Cowhocks or any suggestion of hind leg toeing in or out are faults.*

Sometimes it is difficult to assess the movement of a Maltese in full coat. However, an educated eye can usually spot some of the serious faults, such as dogs with limited reach and drive—demonstrated by an appearance of wasted energy in their locomotion. Other faults to look for include paddling (swinging the front legs forward in a stiff arc) and crabbing (moving with body at an angle) of the front, single tracking of the rear legs and hopping. Hopping can be suggestive of problems with loose kneecaps or loose knee joints on the rear legs.

The Maltese is gentle mannered, yet vigorous and playful.

TEMPERAMENT—*For all her diminutive size, the Maltese seems to be without fear. Her trust and affectionate responsiveness are very appealing. She is among the gentlest mannered of all little dogs, yet she is lively and playful as well as vigorous.*

The temperament of the Maltese is probably one of her most outstanding characteristics. A Maltese that is shy or overly aggressive should be considered to have a serious personality defect.

Standard approved March 10, 1964.

57

CHAPTER SEVEN

A Matter of Fact

Known to many as "ye ancient dogee of Malta," the Maltese can be traced back many centuries. This beautiful, silky-coated, little white dog has a rich and exciting history. The admirers of Maltese come from all walks of life, from the pet fanciers and show fanciers to the rich and famous. Few breeds have achieved such affection and admiration over the years as the elegant little Maltese.

EARLY HISTORY

Many believe that the Maltese originated on the Isle of Malta in the Mediterranean Sea. However, it is argued in Miki Iveria's *The Jewels of*

Women (published by the Maltese Club of Great Britain) and other sources that the Maltese actually originated in Asia. Evidence of dogs resembling the Maltese have been found in ancient drawings, art and writings from as early as 5000 to 2000 B.C.

Assuming the place of origin of the Maltese to be Asia, the tiny dogs probably made their way to Europe through the Middle East with the migration of nomadic tribes. The Isle of Malta (or Melita as it was know then) was a geographic center of early trade, and explorers undoubtedly found ancestors of the tiny white dogs left there as barter for necessities and supplies.

References to the tiny white dog are made in early European writing. In describing a breed of small dogs, Aristotle likens them to the "*Canis Melitae . . .* of the tiny sort, being perfectly proportioned not with-standing its very small rise." The Maltese were favorites of the Greeks and Romans of old. There are many drawings in existence portraying small, longhaired dogs on pieces of Greek and Roman pottery. During these times, the Maltese was a favorite lapdog of fashionable men and women about town, being car-ried wherever its master went.

The ancient Europeans long held the belief that the small dogs came from one of the small islands off the coast of Sicily, hence the name *Canis Melitae.* The island was named both Melita and Malta at that time, and eventually geogra-phers and writers agreed to the name Malta. The Maltese is one of

WHERE DID DOGS COME FROM?

It can be argued that dogs were right there at man's side from the beginning of time. As soon as human beings began to document their existence, the dog was among their drawings and inscriptions. Dogs were not just friends, they served a purpose: There were dogs to hunt birds, pull sleds, herd sheep, burrow after rats—even sit in laps! What your dog was originally bred to do influences the way he behaves. The American Kennel Club recognizes over 140 breeds, and there are hundreds more distinct breeds around the world. To make sense of the breeds, they are grouped according to their size or function. The AKC has seven groups:

1. Sporting
2. Working
3. Herding
4. Hounds
5. Terriers
6. Toys
7. Non Sporting

Can you name a breed from each group? Here's some help: (1) Golden Retriever; (2) Doberman Pinscher; (3) Collie; (4) Beagle; (5) Scottish Terrier; (6) Maltese; and (7) Dalmatian. All modern domestic dogs (*Canis familiaris*) are related, however different they look, and are all descended from *Canis lupus,* the gray wolf.

The admirers of Maltese range from the pet fanciers and show fanciers to the rich and famous.

60

The Maltese was a favorite lapdog among Greek and Roman men and women.

few dog breeds to have retained its name from its known origins.

Malta's location made it an important place in the Mediterranean. It developed a culture and a race of people with distinctive characteristics, and it developed the little Maltese, a race of dogs that differs from almost every other breed. Malta's geographic situation provided an ecology that remained undiluted by outside influences for many centuries. Maltese, as dwellers of the island of Malta, were bred as purebred dogs as far back as the early 1500s.

Maltese were first imported into Britain during the reign of Henry VIII, and they became great favorites in the time of Queen Elizabeth I. By the middle of the nineteenth century, the breed was well established as a pet dog in Britain, and when dog shows began, the Maltese were featured among the early exhibits. Many of the Maltese in the U.S. today trace their heritage back to English imports.

THE MALTESE IN THE UNITED STATES

Maltese were first seen in the United States around the late 1800s, but the geographic origin of these dogs is unknown. We do know, however, that the Maltese lines in the U.S. today resulted from the importation of the breed from Great Britain, Canada, Germany, France

Some experts contend that the elegant Maltese was brought to the Mediterranean from Asia.

FAMOUS OWNERS OF MALTESE

Elizabeth Taylor	Totie Fields
Liberace	John Davidson
Billy Ray Cyrus	Lee Remick
Tara Lipinski	Mia Farrow

The Maltese is an easy breed to train. This dog obeys his owner's "sit" command.

and Italy. Members of the breed were participants in the earliest versions of the Westminster Kennel Club shows in the 1870s. Registrations with the American Kennel Club studbook in that time frame were made on the basis of show winnings.

THE MALTESE IS AN EASY BREED TO TRAIN

Maltese are seen less frequently in AKC Obedience competition than conformation events. Nonetheless, they are an easy breed to train and many owners have enjoyed the competition of earning a CD (Companion Dog) title and CDX (Companion Dog Excellent) title.

CHAPTER EIGHT

On Good Behavior

by Ian Dunbar, Ph.D., MRCVS

Training is the jewel in the crown—the most important aspect of doggy husbandry. There is no more important variable influencing dog behavior and temperament than the dog's education: A well-trained, well-behaved and good-natured puppydog is always a joy to live with, but an untrained and uncivilized dog can be a perpetual nightmare. Moreover, deny the dog an education and she will not have the opportunity to fulfill her own canine potential; neither will she have the ability to

communicate effectively with her human companions.

Luckily, modern psychological training methods are easy, efficient, effective and, above all, considerably dog-friendly and user-friendly. Doggy education is as simple as it is enjoyable. But before you can have a good time play-training with your new dog, you have to learn what to do and how to do it. There is no bigger variable influencing the success of dog training than the owner's experience and expertise. Before you embark on the dog's education, you must first educate yourself.

BASIC TRAINING FOR OWNERS

Ideally, basic owner training should begin well before you select your dog. Find out all you can about your chosen breed first, then master rudimentary training and handling skills. If you already have your puppydog, owner training is a dire emergency—the clock is ticking! Especially for puppies, the first few weeks at home are the most important and influential days in the dog's life. Indeed, the cause of most adolescent and adult problems may be traced back to the initial days the

pup explores her new home. This is the time to establish the *status quo*—to teach the puppydog how you would like her to behave and so prevent otherwise quite predictable problems.

In addition to consulting breeders and breed books such as this one (which understandably have a positive breed bias), seek out as many pet owners with your breed as you can find. Good points are obvious. What you want to find out are the breed-specific problems, so you can nip them in the bud. In particular, you should talk to owners with adolescent dogs and make a list of all anticipated problems. Most important, test drive at least half a dozen adolescent and adult dogs of your breed yourself. An 8-week-old puppy is deceptively easy to handle, but she will acquire adult size, speed and strength in just four months, so you should learn now what to prepare for.

Puppy and pet dog training classes offer a convenient venue to locate pet owners and observe dogs in action. For a list of suitable trainers in your area, contact the Association of Pet Dog Trainers (see chapter 9). You may also begin your basic owner training by observing other owners in class. Watch as many classes and test drive as many dogs as possible. Select an upbeat, dog-friendly, people-friendly, fun-and-games, puppydog pet training class to learn the ropes. Also, watch training videos and read training books. You must find out what to do and how to do it *before* you have to do it.

PRINCIPLES OF TRAINING

Most people think training comprises teaching the dog to do things such as sit, speak and roll over, but even a 4-week-old pup knows how to do these things already. Instead, the first step in training involves teaching the dog human words for each dog behavior and activity and for each aspect of the dog's environment. That way you, the owner, can more easily participate in the dog's domestic education by directing her to perform specific actions appropriately, that is, at the right time, in the right place and so on. Training opens communication channels, enabling an educated dog to at least understand her owner's requests.

In addition to teaching a dog what we want her to do, it is also

OWNING A PARTY ANIMAL

It's a fact: The more of the world your puppy is exposed to, the more comfortable she'll be in it. Once your puppy's had her shots, start taking her everywhere with you. Encourage friendly interaction with strangers, expose her to different environments (towns, fields, beaches) and most important, enroll her in a puppy class where she'll get to play with other puppies. These simple, fun, shared activities will develop your pup into a confident socialite; reliable around other people and dogs.

necessary to teach her why she should do what we ask. Indeed, 95 percent of training revolves around motivating the dog to want to do what we want. Dogs often understand what their owners want; they just don't see the point of doing it—especially when the owner's repetitively boring and seemingly senseless instructions are totally at odds with much more pressing and exciting doggy distractions. It is not so much the dog that is being stubborn or dominant; rather, it is the owner who has failed to acknowledge the dog's needs and feelings and to approach training from the dog's point of view.

65

The Meaning of Instructions

The secret to successful training is learning how to use training lures to predict or prompt specific behaviors—to coax the dog to do what you want when you want. Any highly valued object (such as a treat or toy) may be used as a lure, which the dog will follow with her eyes and nose. Moving the lure in specific ways entices the dog to move her nose, head and entire body in specific ways. In fact, by learning the art of manipulating various lures, it is possible to teach the dog to assume virtually any body position and perform any action. Once you have control over the expression of the dog's behaviors and can elicit any body position or behavior at will, you can easily teach the dog to perform on request.

Tell your dog what you want her to do, use a lure to entice her to respond correctly, then profusely praise and maybe reward her once she performs the desired action. For example, verbally request "Fido, sit!" while you move a squeaky toy upwards and backwards over the dog's muzzle (lure-movement and hand signal), smile knowingly as she looks up (to follow the lure) and sits down (as a result of canine anatomical engineering), then praise her to distraction ("Gooood Fido!").

Knowing what to expect of your puppy prior to her arrival in your home is a great way to stop behavior problems before they start.

Squeak the toy, offer a training treat and give your dog and yourself a pat on the back.

Being able to elicit desired responses over and over enables the owner to reward the dog over and over. Consequently, the dog begins to think training is fun. For example, the more the dog is rewarded for sitting, the more she enjoys sitting. Eventually the dog comes to realize that, whereas most sitting is appreciated, sitting immediately upon request usually prompts especially enthusiastic praise and a slew of high-level rewards. The dog begins to sit on cue much of the time, showing that she is starting to grasp the meaning of the owner's verbal request and hand signal.

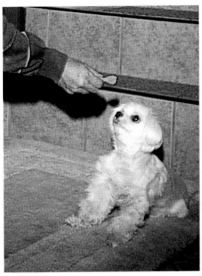

You can quickly train your dog to do virtually anything when using the lure-reward method, and it is enjoyable for dogs, too!

Why Comply?

Most dogs enjoy initial lure-reward training and are only too happy to comply with their owners' wishes. Unfortunately, repetitive drilling without appreciative feedback tends to diminish the dog's enthusiasm until she eventually fails to see the point of complying anymore. Moreover, as the dog approaches adolescence she becomes more easily distracted as she develops other interests. Lengthy sessions with repetitive exercises tend to bore and demotivate both parties. If it's not fun, the owner doesn't do it and neither does the dog.

Integrate training into your dog's life: The greater number of training sessions each day and the shorter they are, the more willingly compliant your dog will become. Make sure to have a short (just a few seconds) training interlude before every enjoyable canine activity. For example, ask your dog to sit to greet people, to sit before you throw her Frisbee and to sit for her supper. Really, sitting is no different from a canine "Please." Also, include numerous short training interludes during every enjoyable canine pastime, for example, when playing with the dog or when she is running in the park. In this fashion, doggy distractions may be effectively converted into rewards for training. Just as all games have rules, fun becomes training . . . and training becomes fun.

Eventually, rewards actually become unnecessary to continue motivating your dog. If trained with consideration and kindness, performing the desired behaviors will become self-rewarding and, in a sense, your dog will motivate herself. Just as it is not necessary to reward a human companion during an enjoyable walk in the park, or following a game of tennis, it is hardly necessary to reward our best friend—the

Punishment training does not stop your pet from misbehaving. Instead, it teaches your pet to perform the action when (or where) you can't see it.

dog—for walking by our side or while playing fetch. Human company during enjoyable activities is reward enough for most dogs.

Even though your dog has become self-motivating, it's still good to praise and pet her a lot and offer rewards once in a while, especially for a good job well done. And if for no other reason, praising and rewarding others is good for the human heart.

Punishment

Without a doubt, lure-reward training is by far the best way to teach: Entice your dog to do what you want and then reward her for doing so. Unfortunately, a human shortcoming is to take the good for granted and to moan and groan at the bad. Specifically, the dog's many good behaviors are ignored while the owner focuses on punishing the dog for making mistakes. In extreme cases, instruction is limited to punishing mistakes made by a trainee dog, child, employee or husband, even though it has been proven punishment training is notoriously inefficient and ineffective and is decidedly unfriendly and combative. It teaches the dog that training is a

drag, almost as quickly as it teaches the dog to dislike her trainer. Why treat our best friends like our worst enemies?

Punishment training is also much more laborious and time consuming. Whereas it takes only a finite amount of time to teach a dog what to chew, for example, it takes much, much longer to punish the dog for each and every mistake. Remember, there is only one right way! So why not teach that right way from the outset?!

To make matters worse, punishment training causes severe lapses in the dog's reliability. Since it is obviously impossible to punish the dog each and every time she misbehaves, the dog quickly learns to distinguish between those times when she must comply (so as to avoid impending punishment) and those times when she need not comply, because punishment is impossible. Such times include when the dog is off leash and 6 feet away, when the owner is otherwise engaged (talking to a friend, watching television, taking a shower, tending to the baby or chatting on the telephone) or when the dog is left at home alone.

Instances of misbehavior will be numerous when the owner is away,

because even when the dog complied in the owner's looming presence, she did so unwillingly. The dog was forced to act against her will, rather than molding her will to want to please. Hence, when the owner is absent, not only does the dog know she need not comply, she simply does not want to. Again, the trainee is not a stubborn vindictive beast, but rather the trainer has failed to teach. Punishment training invariably creates unpredictable Jekyll and Hyde behavior.

TRAINER'S TOOLS

Many training books extol the virtues of a vast array of training paraphernalia and electronic and metallic gizmos, most of which are designed for canine restraint, correction and punishment, rather than for actual facilitation of doggy education. In reality, most effective training tools are not found in stores; they come from within ourselves. In addition to a willing dog, all you really need is a functional human brain, gentle hands, a loving heart and a good attitude.

In terms of equipment, all dogs do require a quality buckle collar to sport dog tags and to attach the

69

leash (for safety and to comply with local leash laws). Hollow chew toys (like Kongs or sterilized longbones) and a dog bed or collapsible crate are musts for housetraining. Three additional tools are required:

1. specific lures (training treats and toys) to predict and prompt specific desired behaviors;

2. rewards (praise, affection, training treats and toys) to reinforce for the dog what a lot of fun it all is; and

3. knowledge—how to convert the dog's favorite activities and games (potential distractions to training) into "life-rewards," which may be employed to facilitate training.

The most powerful of these is knowledge. Education is the key! Watch training classes, participate in training classes, watch videos, read books, enjoy play-training with your dog and then your dog will say "Please," and your dog will say "Thank you!"

HOUSETRAINING

If dogs were left to their own devices, certainly they would chew, dig and bark for entertainment and then no doubt highlight a few areas of their living space with sprinkles of urine, in much the same way we decorate by hanging pictures. Consequently, when we ask a dog to live with us, we must teach her *where* she may dig, *where* she may perform her toilet duties, *what* she may chew and *when* she may bark. After all, when left at home alone for many hours, we cannot expect the dog to amuse herself by completing crosswords or watching the soaps on TV!

Also, it would be decidedly unfair to keep the house rules a secret from the dog, and then get angry and punish the poor critter for inevitably transgressing rules she did not even know existed. Remember: Without adequate education and guidance, the dog will be forced to establish her own rules—doggy rules—and most probably will be at odds with the owner's view of domestic living.

Since most problems develop during the first few days the dog is at home, prospective dog owners must be certain they are quite clear about the principles of housetraining *before* they get a dog. Early misbehaviors quickly become established as the *status quo*—becoming firmly entrenched as hard-to-break bad habits, which set the precedent for years to come. Make sure to teach your dog good habits right from the start. Good habits are just as hard to break as bad ones!

Ideally, when a new dog comes home, try to arrange for someone to be present as much as possible during the first few days (for adult dogs) or weeks for puppies. With only a little forethought, it is surprisingly easy to find a puppy sitter, such as a retired person, who would be willing to eat from your refrigerator and watch your television while keeping an eye on the newcomer to encourage the dog to play with chew toys and to ensure she goes outside on a regular basis.

Potty Training

To teach the dog where to relieve herself:

1. never let her make a single mistake;

2. let her know where you want her to go; and

3. handsomely reward her for doing so: "GOOOOOOOD DOG!!!" liver treat, liver treat, liver treat!

HOUSETRAINING 1-2-3

1. Prevent Mistakes. When you can't supervise your puppy, confine her in a single room or in her crate (but don't leave her for too long!). Puppy-proof the area by laying down newspapers so that if she does make a mistake, it won't matter.

2. Teach Where. Take your puppy to the spot you want her to use every hour.

3. When she goes, praise her profusely and give her three favorite treats.

71

Preventing Mistakes

A single mistake is a training disaster, since it heralds many more in future weeks. And each time the dog soils the house, this further reinforces the dog's unfortunate preference for an indoor, carpeted toilet. Do not let an unhousetrained dog have full run of the house.

When you are away from home, or cannot pay full attention, confine the dog to an area where elimination is appropriate, such as an outdoor run or, better still, a small, comfortable indoor kennel with access to an outdoor run. When confined in this manner, most dogs will naturally housetrain themselves.

If that's not possible, confine the dog to an area, such as a utility room, kitchen, basement or garage, where elimination may not be desired in the long run but as an interim measure it is certainly preferable to doing it all around the house. Use newspaper to cover the floor of the dog's day room. The newspaper may be used to soak up the urine and to wrap up and dispose of the feces. Once your dog develops a preferred spot for eliminating, it is only necessary to cover that part of the floor with newspaper. The smaller papered area may then be moved (only a little each day) towards the door to the outside. Thus the dog will develop the tendency to go to the door when she needs to relieve herself.

Never confine an unhousetrained dog to a crate for long periods. Doing so would force the dog to soil the crate and ruin its usefulness as an aid for housetraining (see the following discussion).

Teaching Where

In order to teach your dog where you would like her to do her business, you have to be there to direct the proceedings—an obvious,

yet often neglected, fact of life. In order to be there to teach the dog where to go, you need to know *when* she needs to go. Indeed, the success of housetraining depends on the owner's ability to predict these times. Certainly, a regular feeding schedule will facilitate prediction somewhat, but there is nothing like "loading the deck" and influencing the timing of the outcome yourself!

Whenever you are at home, make sure the dog is under constant supervision and/or confined to a small area. If already well trained, simply instruct the dog to lie down in her bed or basket. Alternatively, confine the dog to a crate (doggy den) or tie-down (a short, 18-inch lead that can be clipped to an eye hook in the baseboard near her bed). Short-term close confinement strongly inhibits urination and defecation, since the dog does not want to soil her sleeping area. Thus, when you release the puppydog each hour, she will definitely need to urinate immediately and defecate every third or fourth hour. Keep the dog confined to her doggy den and take her to her intended toilet area each hour, every hour and on the hour. When taking your dog outside, instruct her to sit quietly before opening the door—she will soon learn to sit by the door when she needs to go out!

Teaching Why

Being able to predict when the dog needs to go enables the owner to be on the spot to praise and reward the dog. Each hour, hurry the dog to the intended toilet area in the yard, issue the appropriate instruction ("Go pee!" or "Go poop!"), then give the dog three to four minutes to produce. Praise and offer a couple of training treats when successful. The treats are important because many people fail to praise their dogs with feeling . . . and housetraining is hardly the time for understatement. So either loosen up and enthusiastically praise that dog: "Wuzzzer-wuzzer-wuzzer, hoooser good wuffer den? Hoooo went pee for Daddy?" Or say "Good dog!" as best you can and offer the treats for effect.

Following elimination is an ideal time for a spot of play-training in the yard or house. Also, an empty dog may be allowed greater freedom around the house for the next half hour or so, just as long as you keep an eye out to make sure she does not get into other kinds of mischief. If you are preoccupied and cannot pay full attention, confine the dog to her doggy den once more to enjoy a peaceful snooze or to play with her many chew toys.

If your dog does not eliminate within the allotted time outside—no biggie! Back to her doggy den, and then try again after another hour.

As I own large dogs, I always feel more relaxed walking an empty dog, knowing that I will not need to finish our stroll weighted down with bags of feces!

Beware of falling into the trap of walking the dog to get her to eliminate. The good ol' dog walk is such an enormous highlight in the dog's life that it represents the single biggest potential reward in domestic dogdom. However, when in a hurry, or during inclement weather, many owners abruptly terminate the walk the moment the dog has done her business. This, in effect, severely punishes the dog for doing the right thing, in the right place at the right time. Consequently, many dogs become strongly inhibited from eliminating outdoors because they know it will signal an abrupt end to an otherwise thoroughly enjoyable walk.

TOYS THAT EARN THEIR KEEP

To entertain even the most distracted of dogs, while you're home or away, have a selection of the following toys on hand: hollow chew toys (like Kongs, sterilized hollow longbones and cubes or balls that can be stuffed with kibble). Smear peanut butter or honey on the inside of the hollow toy or bone, stuff the bone with kibble and your dog will think of nothing else but working the object to get at the food. Great to take your dog's mind off the fact that you've left the house.

Instead, instruct the dog to relieve herself in the yard prior to going for a walk. If you follow the above instructions, most dogs soon learn to eliminate on cue. As soon as the dog eliminates, praise (and offer a treat or two)—"Good dog! Let's go walkies!" Use the walk as a reward for eliminating in the yard. If the dog does not go, put her back in her doggy den and think about a walk later on. You will find with a "No feces—no walk" policy, your dog will become one of the fastest defecators in the business.

If you do not have a backyard, instruct the dog to eliminate right outside your front door prior to the walk. Not only will this facilitate clean up and disposal of the feces in your own trash can but, also, the walk may again be used as a colossal reward.

CHEWING AND BARKING

Short-term close confinement also teaches the dog that occasional quiet moments are a reality of domestic living. Your puppydog is extremely impressionable during her first few weeks at home. Regular confinement at this time soon exerts a calming influence over the dog's personality. Remember, once the dog is housetrained and calmer, there will be a whole lifetime ahead for the dog to enjoy full run of the house and garden. On the other hand, by letting the newcomer have unrestricted access to the entire household and allowing her to run willy-nilly, she will most certainly develop a bunch of behavior problems in short order, no doubt necessitating confinement later in life. It would not be fair to remedially restrain and confine a dog you have trained, through neglect, to run free.

When confining the dog, make sure she always has an impressive array of suitable chew toys. Kongs and sterilized longbones (both read-ily available from pet stores) make the best chew toys, since they are hollow and may be stuffed with treats to heighten the dog's interest. For example, by stuffing the little hole at the top of a Kong with a small piece of freeze-dried liver, the dog will not want to leave it alone.

Remember, treats do not have to be junk food and they certainly should not represent extra calories. Rather, treats should be part of each dog's regular daily diet: Some food may be served in the dog's bowl for breakfast and dinner, some food may be used as training treats, and some food may be used for stuffing chew toys. I regularly stuff my dogs' many Kongs with different shaped biscuits and kibble. The kibble seems to fall out fairly easily, as do the oval-shaped biscuits, thus rewarding the dog instantaneously for checking out the chew toys. The bone-shaped biscuits fall out after a while, rewarding the dog for worrying at the chew toy. But the triangular biscuits never come out. They remain inside the Kong as lures, maintaining the dog's fascination with her chew toy. To further focus the dog's interest, I always make sure to flavor the trian-gular biscuits by rubbing them with a little cheese or freeze-dried liver.

Teaching your puppy to play with lots of fun toys will keep her from chew-ing up your shoes, and will certainly remain your pet's favorite hobby into her adult years.

If stuffed chew toys are reserved especially for times the dog is confined, the puppydog will soon learn to enjoy quiet moments in her doggy den and she will quickly develop a chew-toy habit—a good habit! This is a simple autoshaping process; all the owner has to do is set up the situation and the dog all but trains herself—easy and effective. Even when the dog is given run of the house, her first inclination will be to indulge her rewarding chew-toy habit rather than destroy less-attractive household articles, such as curtains, carpets, chairs and compact disks. Similarly, a chew-toy chewer will be less inclined to scratch and chew herself excessively. Also, if the dog busies herself as a recreational chewer, she will be less inclined to develop into a recreational barker or digger when left at home alone.

Stuff a number of chew toys whenever the dog is left confined and remove the extra-special-tasting treats when you return. Your dog will now amuse herself with her chew toys before falling asleep and then resume playing with her chew toys when she expects you to return. Since most owner-absent misbehavior happens right after you leave and

right before your expected return, your puppydog will now be conveniently preoccupied with her chew toys at these times.

COME AND SIT

Most puppies will happily approach virtually anyone, whether called or not; that is, until they collide with adolescence and develop other more important doggy interests, such as sniffing a multiplicity of exquisite odors on the grass.

Your mission, Mr./Ms. Owner, is to teach and reward the pup for coming reliably, willingly and happily when called—and you have just three months to get it done. Unless adequately reinforced, your puppy's tendency to approach people will self-destruct by adolescence.

Call your dog ("Fido, come!"), open your arms (and maybe squat down) as a welcoming signal, waggle a treat or toy as a lure and reward the puppydog when she comes running. Do not wait to praise the dog until she reaches you—she may come 95 percent of the way and then run off after some distraction. Instead, praise the dog's first step towards you and continue praising enthusiastically for every step she takes in your direction.

When the rapidly approaching puppy dog is three lengths away from impact, instruct her to sit ("Fido, sit!") and hold the lure in front of you in an outstretched hand to prevent her from hitting you mid-chest and knocking you flat on your back! As Fido decelerates to nose the lure, move the treat upwards and backwards just over her muzzle with an upwards motion of your extended arm (palm-upwards). As the dog looks up to follow the lure, she will sit down (if she jumps up, you are holding the lure too high). Praise the dog for sitting. Move backwards and call her again. Repeat this many times over, always praising when Fido comes and sits; on occasion, reward her.

For the first couple of trials, use a training treat both as a lure to entice the dog to come and sit and as a reward for doing so. Thereafter, try to use different items as lures and rewards. For example, lure the dog with a Kong or Frisbee but reward her with a food treat. Or lure the dog with a food treat but pat her and throw a tennis ball as a reward. After just a few repetitions, dispense with the lures and rewards; the dog

will begin to respond willingly to your verbal requests and hand signals just for the prospect of praise from your heart and affection from your hands.

Instruct every family member, friend and visitor how to get the dog to come and sit. Invite people over for a series of pooch parties; do not keep the pup a secret—let other people enjoy this puppy, and let the pup enjoy other people. Puppydog parties are not only fun, they easily attract a lot of people to help you train your dog. Unless you teach your dog how to meet people, that is, to sit for greetings, no doubt the dog will resort to jumping up. Then you and the visitors will get annoyed, and the dog will be punished. This is not fair. Send out those invitations for puppy parties and teach your dog to be mannerly and socially acceptable.

Even though your dog quickly masters obedient recalls in the house, her reliability may falter when playing in the backyard or local park. Ironically, it is the owner who has unintentionally trained the dog not to respond in these instances. By allowing the dog to play and run around and otherwise have a good time, but then to call

This owner has taught her Maltese that training is fun.

dog enthusiastically before releasing her. The dog will learn that coming when called is not necessarily the end of the play session, and neither is it the end of the world; rather, it signals an enjoyable, quality time-out with the owner before resuming play once more. In fact, playing in the park now becomes a very effective life-reward, which works to facilitate training by reinforcing each obedient and timely recall. Good news!

SIT, DOWN, STAND AND ROLLOVER

Teaching the dog a variety of body positions is easy for owner and dog, impressive for spectators and extremely useful for all. Using lure-reward techniques, it is possible to train several positions at once to verbal commands or hand signals (which impress the socks off onlookers).

Sit and down—the two control commands—prevent or resolve nearly a hundred behavior problems. For example, if the dog happily and obediently sits or lies down when requested, she cannot jump on visitors, dash out the front door, run around and chase her tail, pester

the dog to put her on leash to take her home, the dog quickly learns playing is fun but training is a drag. Thus, playing in the park becomes a severe distraction, which works against training. Bad news!

Instead, whether playing with the dog off leash or on leash, request her to come at frequent intervals—say, every minute or so. On most occasions, praise and pet the dog for a few seconds while she is sitting, then tell her to go play again. For especially fast recalls, offer a couple of training treats and take the time to praise and pet the other dogs, harass cats or annoy family, friends or strangers. Additionally, "Sit" or "Down" are the best emergency commands for off-leash control.

It is easier to teach and maintain a reliable sit than maintain a reliable recall. Sit is the purest and simplest of commands—either the dog is sitting or she is not. If there is any change of circumstances or potential danger in the park, for example, simply instruct the dog to sit. If she sits, you have a number of options: Allow the dog to resume playing when she is safe, walk up and put the dog on leash or call the dog. The dog will be much more likely to come when called if she has already acknowledged her compliance by sitting. If the dog does not sit in the park—train her to!

Stand and rollover-stay are the two positions for examining the dog. Your veterinarian will love you to distraction if you take a little time to teach the dog to stand still and roll over and play possum. Also, your vet bills will be smaller because it will take the veterinarian less time to examine your dog. The rollover-stay is an especially useful command and is really just a variation of the down-stay: Whereas the dog lies prone in

the traditional down, she lies supine in the rollover-stay.

As with teaching come and sit, the training techniques to teach the dog to assume all other body positions on cue are user-friendly and dog-friendly. Simply give the appropriate request, lure the dog into the desired body position using a training treat or toy and then praise (and maybe reward) the dog as soon as she complies. Try not to touch the dog to get her to respond. If you teach the dog by guiding her into position, the dog will quickly learn that rump-pressure means sit, for example, but as yet you still have no control over your dog if she is just 6 feet away. It will still be necessary to teach the dog to sit on request. So do not make training a time-consuming two-step process; instead, teach the dog to sit to a verbal request or hand signal from the outset. Once the dog sits willingly when requested, by all means use your hands to pet the dog when she does so.

To teach down when the dog is already sitting, say "Fido, down!," hold the lure in one hand (palm down) and lower that hand to the floor between the dog's forepaws. As the dog lowers her head to follow the lure, slowly move the lure away from the dog just a fraction (in front of her paws). The dog will lie down as she stretches her nose forward to follow the lure. Praise the dog when she does so. If the dog stands up, you pulled the lure away too far and too quickly.

When teaching the dog to lie down from the standing position, say "Down" and lower the lure to the floor as before. Once the dog has lowered her forequarters and assumed a play bow, gently and slowly move the lure towards the dog between her forelegs. Praise the dog as soon as her rear end plops down.

After just a couple of trials it will be possible to alternate sits and downs and have the dog energetically perform doggy push-ups. Praise the dog a lot, and after half a dozen or so push-ups reward the dog with a training treat or toy. You will notice the more energetically you move your arm—upwards (palm up) to get the dog to sit, and downwards (palm down) to get the dog to lie down—the more energetically the dog responds to your requests. Now try training the dog in silence and you will notice she has also learned to respond to hand signals. Yeah! Not too shabby for the first session.

To teach stand from the sitting position, say "Fido, stand," slowly move the lure half a dog-length away from the dog's nose, keeping it at nose level, and praise the dog as she stands to follow the lure. As soon as the dog stands, lower the lure to just beneath the dog's chin to entice her to look down; otherwise she will stand and then sit immediately. To prompt the dog to stand from the down position, move the lure half a dog-length upwards and away from the dog, holding the lure at standing nose height from the floor.

Teaching rollover is best started from the down position, with the dog lying on one side, or at least with both hind legs stretched out on the same side. Say "Fido, bang!" and move the lure backwards and alongside the dog's muzzle to her elbow (on the side of her outstretched hind legs). Once the dog looks to the side and backwards, very slowly move the lure upwards to the dog's shoulder and backbone. Tickling the dog in the goolies (groin area) often invokes a reflex-raising of the hind leg as an appeasement gesture, which facilitates the tendency to roll over. If you move the lure too quickly and the dog jumps into the standing position, have patience and start again. As soon as the dog rolls onto her back, keep the lure stationary and mesmerize the dog with a relaxing tummy rub.

To teach rollover-stay when the dog is standing or moving, say "Fido, bang!" and give the appropriate hand signal (with index finger pointed and thumb cocked in true Sam Spade fashion), then in one fluid movement lure her to first lie down and then rollover-stay as above.

Teaching the dog to stay in each of the above four positions becomes a piece of cake after first teaching the dog not to worry at the toy or treat training lure. This is best accomplished by hand feeding dinner kibble. Hold a piece of kibble firmly in your hand and softly instruct "Off!" Ignore any licking and slobbering for however long the dog worries at the treat, but say "Take it!" and offer the kibble *the instant* the dog breaks contact with her muzzle. Repeat this a few times, and then up the ante and insist the dog remove her muzzle for one whole second before offering the kibble. Then progressively refine your criteria and have the dog not touch your hand (or treat) for longer and longer periods on each trial, such as for two seconds, four

seconds, then six, ten, fifteen, twenty, thirty seconds and so on.

The dog soon learns: (1) worrying at the treat never gets results, whereas (2) noncontact is often rewarded after a variable time lapse.

Teaching "Off!" has many useful applications in its own right. Additionally, instructing the dog not to touch a training lure often produces spontaneous and magical stays. Request the dog to stand-stay, for example, and not to touch the lure. At first set your sights on a short two-second stay before rewarding the dog. (Remember, every long journey begins with a single step.) However, on subsequent trials, gradually and progressively increase the length of stay required to receive a reward. In no time at all your dog will stand calmly for a minute or so.

RELEVANCY TRAINING

Once you have taught the dog what you expect her to do when requested to come, sit, lie down, stand, rollover and stay, the time is right to teach the dog why she should comply with your wishes. The secret is to have many (many) extremely short

81

training interludes (two to five seconds each) at numerous (numerous) times during the course of the dog's day. Especially work with the dog immediately before the dog's good times and during the dog's good times. For example, ask your dog to sit and/or lie down each time before opening doors, serving meals, offering treats and tummy rubs; ask the dog to perform a few controlled doggy push-ups before letting her off leash or throwing a tennis ball; and perhaps request the dog to sit-down-sit-stand-down-stand-rollover before inviting her to cuddle on the couch.

This Maltese has learned to tell her owner when she has to relieve herself.

Similarly, request the dog to sit many times during play or on walks, and in no time at all the dog will be only too pleased to follow your instructions because she has learned that a compliant response heralds all sorts of goodies. Basically all you are trying to teach the dog is how to say please: "Please throw the tennis ball. Please may I snuggle on the couch."

Remember, it is important to keep training interludes short and to have many short sessions each and every day. The shortest (and most useful) session comprises asking the dog to sit and then go play during a play session. When trained this way, your dog will soon associate training with good times. In fact, the dog may be unable to distinguish between training and good times and, indeed, there should be no distinction. The warped concept that training involves forcing the dog to comply and/or dominating her will is totally at odds with the picture of a truly well-trained dog. In reality, enjoying a game of training with a dog is no different from enjoying a game of backgammon or tennis with a friend; and walking with a dog should be no different from strolling with a spouse, or with buddies on the golf course.

WALK BY YOUR SIDE

Many people attempt to teach a dog to heel by putting her on a leash and physically correcting the dog when she makes mistakes. There are a number of things seriously wrong with this approach, the first being that most people do not want precision heeling; rather, they simply want the dog to follow or walk by their side. Second, when physically restrained during "training," even though the dog may grudgingly mope by your side when "hand-cuffed" on leash, let's see what happens when she is off leash. History! The dog is in the next county because she never enjoyed walking with you on leash and you have no control over her off leash. So let's just teach the dog off leash from the outset to want to walk with us. Third, if the dog has not been trained to heel, it is a trifle hasty to think about punishing the poor dog for making mistakes and breaking heeling rules she didn't even know existed. This is simply not fair! Surely, if the dog had been adequately taught how to heel, she would seldom make mistakes and hence there would be no need to

FINDING A TRAINER

Have fun with your dog, take a training class! But don't just sign on any dotted line, find a trainer whose approach and style you like and whose students (and their dogs) are really learning. Ask to visit a class to observe a trainer in action. For the names of trainers near you, ask your veterinarian, your pet supply store, your dog-owning neighbors or call (800) PET-DOGS (the Association of Pet Dog Trainers.)

correct the dog. Remember, each mistake and each correction (punishment) advertise the trainer's inadequacy, not the dog's. The dog is not stubborn, she is not stupid and she is not bad. Even if she were, she would still require training, so let's train her properly.

Let's teach the dog to enjoy following us and to want to walk by our side off leash. Then it will be easier to teach high-precision off-leash heeling patterns if desired. Before going on outdoor walks, it is necessary to teach the dog not to pull. Then it becomes easy to teach on-leash walking and heeling because the dog already wants to walk with you, she is familiar with the desired walking and heeling positions and she knows not to pull.

83

FOLLOWING

Start by training your dog to follow you. Many puppies will follow if you simply walk away from them and maybe click your fingers or chuckle. Adult dogs may require additional enticement to stimulate them to follow, such as a training lure or, at the very least, a lively trainer. To teach the dog to follow: (1) keep walking and (2) walk away from the dog. If the dog attempts to lead or lag, change pace; slow down if the dog forges too far ahead, but speed up if she lags too far behind. Say "Steady!" or "Easy!" each time before you slow down and "Quickly!" or "Hustle!" each time before you speed up, and the dog will learn to change pace on cue. If the dog lags or leads too far, or if she wanders right or left, simply walk quickly in the opposite direction and maybe even run away from the dog and hide.

Practicing is a lot of fun; you can set up a course in your home, yard or park to do this. Indoors, entice the dog to follow upstairs, into a bedroom, into the bathroom, downstairs, around the living room couch, zigzagging between dining room chairs and into the kitchen for dinner. Outdoors, get the dog to follow around park benches, trees, shrubs and along walkways and lines in the grass. (For safety outdoors, it is advisable to attach a long line on the dog, but never exert corrective tension on the line.)

Remember, following has a lot to do with attitude—your attitude! Most probably your dog will not want to follow Mr. Grumpy Troll with the personality of wilted lettuce. Lighten up—walk with a jaunty step, whistle a happy tune, sing, skip and tell jokes to your dog and she will be right there by your side.

84

A well-trained Maltese will walk easily and calmly by your side.

THE IMPORTANCE OF TRICKS

Nothing will improve a dog's quality of life better than having a few tricks under her belt. Teaching any trick expands the dog's vocabulary, which facilitates communication and improves the owner's control. Also, specific tricks help prevent and resolve specific behavior problems. For example, by teaching the dog to fetch her toys, the dog learns carrying a toy makes the owner happy and, therefore, will be more likely to chew her toy than other inappropriate items.

Tricks facilitate training. For example, by the time the owner has enjoyed teaching her dog the "ol' balance the biscuit on the nose" trick, she already has a dynamite sit-stay!

More important, teaching tricks prompts owners to lighten up and train with a sunny disposition. Really, tricks should be no different from any other behaviors we put on cue. But they are. When teaching tricks, owners have a much sweeter attitude, which in turn motivates the dog and improves her willingness to comply. The dog feels tricks are a blast, but formal commands are a drag. In fact, tricks are so enjoyable, they may be used as rewards in training by asking the dog to come, sit and down-stay and then rollover for a tummy rub. Go on, try it: Crack a smile and even giggle when the dog promptly and willingly lies down and stays.

Most important, performing tricks prompts onlookers to smile and giggle. Many people are scared of dogs, especially large ones. And nothing can be more off-putting for a dog than to be constantly confronted by strangers who don't like her because of her size or the way she looks. Uneasy people put the dog on edge, causing her to back off and bark, only frightening people all the more. And so a vicious circle develops, with the people's fear fueling the dog's fear *and vice versa*. Instead, tie a pink ribbon to your dog's collar and practice all sorts of tricks on walks and in the park, and you will be pleasantly amazed how it changes people's attitudes toward your friendly dog.

CHAPTER NINE

Resources

BOOKS

About Maltese

Henrieff, Vicki. *The Maltese Today.* New York: Howell Book House, 1996.

Nicholas, Anna Katherine. *The Maltese.* Neptune, NJ: TFH Publications, 1984.

About Health Care

American Kennel Club. *American Kennel Club Dog Care and Training.* New York: Howell Book House, 1991.

Carlson, Delbert, DVM, and James Giffen, MD. *Dog Owner's Home Veterinary Handbook.* New York: Howell Book House, 1992.

DeBitetto, James, DVM, and Sarah Hodgson. *You & Your Puppy.* New York: Howell Book House, 1995.

Lane, Marion. *The Humane Society of the United States Complete Guide to Dog Care.* New York: Little, Brown & Co., 1998.

McGinnis, Terri. *The Well Dog Book.* New York: Random House, 1991.

Schwartz, Stephanie, DVM. *First Aid for Dogs: An Owner's Guide to a Happy Healthy Pet.* New York: Howell Book House, 1998.

Volhard, Wendy and Kerry L. Brown. *The Holistic Guide for a Healthy Dog.* New York: Howell Book House, 1995.

About Training

Ammen, Amy. *Training in No Time.* New York: Howell Book House, 1995.

Benjamin, Carol Lea. *Mother Knows Best.* New York: Howell Book House, 1985.

Bohnenkamp, Gwen. *Manners for the Modern Dog.* San Francisco: Perfect Paws, 1990.

Dunbar, Ian, Ph.D., MRCVS. *Dr. Dunbar's Good Little Book.* James & Kenneth Publishers, 2140 Shattuck Ave. #2406, Berkeley, CA 94704. (510) 658-8588. Order from Publisher.

Evans, Job Michael. *People, Pooches and Problems.* New York: Howell Book House, 1991.

Palika, Liz. *All Dogs Need Some Training.* New York: Howell Book House, 1997.

Volhard, Jack and Melissa Bartlett. *What All Good Dogs Should Know: The Sensible Way to Train.* New York: Howell Book House, 1991.

About Activities

Hall, Lynn. *Dog Showing for Beginners.* New York: Howell Book House, 1994.

O'Neil, Jackie. *All About Agility.* New York: Howell Book House, 1998.

Simmons-Moake, Jane. *Agility Training, The Fun Sport for All Dogs.* New York: Howell Book House, 1991.

Vanacore, Connie. *Dog Showing: An Owner's Guide.* New York: Howell Book House, 1990.

Volhard, Jack and Wendy. *The Canine Good Citizen.* New York: Howell Book House, 1994.

MAGAZINES

The AKC GAZETTE, The Official Journal for the Sport of Purebred Dogs
American Kennel Club
260 Madison Avenue
New York, NY 10016
www.akc.org

Dog Fancy
Fancy Publications
3 Burroughs
Irvine, CA 92618
(714) 855-8822
http://dogfancy.com

Dog World
Maclean Hunter Publishing Corp.
500 N. Dearborn, Suite 1100
Chicago, IL 60610
(312) 396-0600
www.dogworldmag.com

PetLife: Your Companion Animal Magazine
Magnolia Media Group
1400 Two Tandy Center
Fort Worth, TX 76102
(800) 767-9377
www.petlifeweb.com

Dog & Kennel
7-L Dundas Circle
Greensboro, NC 27407
(336) 292-4047
www.dogandkennel.com

MORE INFORMATION ABOUT BREED

National Breed Club

AMERICAN MALTESE ASSOCIATION
Corresponding Secretary:
   Pamela G. Rightmyer
   2211. S. Tioga Way
   Las Vegas, NV 89117

Breeder Contact:
   Julie Phillips
   3703 SE 17th Avenue
   Cape Coral, FL 33904
   (941) 549-4446

The Club can send you information on all aspects of the breed, including the names and addresses of breed clubs in your area, as well as obedience clubs. Inquire about membership.

The American Kennel Club

The American Kennel Club (AKC), devoted to the advancement of purebred dogs, is the oldest and largest registry organization in this country. Every breed recognized by the AKC has a national (parent) club. National clubs are a great source of information on your breed. The affiliated clubs hold AKC events and use AKC rules to hold performance events, dog shows, educational programs, health clinics and training classes. The AKC staff is divided between offices in New York City and Raleigh, North Carolina. The AKC has an excellent web site that provides information on the organization and all AKC-recognized breeds. The address is www.akc.org.

For registration and performance events information, or for customer service, contact:

THE AMERICAN KENNEL CLUB
5580 Centerview Drive, Suite 200
Raleigh, NC 27606
(919) 233-9767

The AKC's executive offices and the AKC Library (open to the public) are at this address:

THE AMERICAN KENNEL CLUB
260 Madison Avenue
New York, New York 10016
(212) 696-8200 (general information)
(212) 696-8246 (AKC Library)
www.akc.org

UNITED KENNEL CLUB
100 E. Kilgore Road
Kalamazoo, MI 49001-5598
(616) 343-9020
www.ukcdogs.com

AMERICAN RARE BREED ASSOCIATION
9921 Frank Tippett Road
Cheltenham, MD 20623
(301) 868-5718 (voice or fax)
www.arba.org

CANADIAN KENNEL CLUB
89 Skyway Avenue, Suite 100
Etobicoke, Ontario
Canada M9W 6R4
(416) 675-5511
www.ckc.ca

ORTHOPEDIC FOUNDATION FOR ANIMALS (OFA)
2300 E. Nifong Blvd.
Columbia, MO 65201-3856
(314) 442-0418
www.offa.org/

Trainers

Animal Behavior & Training Associates (ABTA)
9018 Balboa Blvd., Suite 591
Northridge, CA 91325
(800) 795-3294
www.Good-dawg.com

Association of Pet Dog Trainers (APDT)
(800) PET-DOGS
www.apdt.com

National Association of Dog Obedience Instructors (NADOI)
729 Grapevine Highway, Suite 369
Hurst, TX 76054-2085
www.kimberly.uidaho.edu/nadoi

Associations

Delta Society
P.O. Box 1080
Renton, WA 98507-1080
(Promotes the human/animal bond
through pet-assisted therapy and other
programs)
**www.petsform.com/DELTASOCIETY/
dsi400.htm**

Dog Writers Association of America
(DWAA)
Sally Cooper, Secretary
222 Woodchuck Lane
Harwinton, CT 06791
www.dwaa.org

National Association for Search and
Rescue (NASAR)
4500 Southgate Place, Suite 100
Chantilly, VA 20157
(703) 222-6277
www.nasar.org

Therapy Dogs International
6 Hilltop Road
Mendham, NJ 07945

OTHER USEFUL RESOURCES—WEB SITES

General Information— Links to Additional Sites, On-Line Shopping

www.k9web.com–resources for the dog
world

www.netpet.com–pet related products,
software and services

www.apapets.com–The American Pet
Association

www.dogandcatbooks.com–book catalog

www.dogbooks.com–on-line bookshop

www.animal.discovery.com/–cable
television channel on-line

Health

www.avma.org–American Veterinary
Medical Association (AVMA)

www.aplb.org–Association for Pet Loss
Bereavement (APLB)—contains an
index of national hot lines for on-line
and office counseling.

**www.netfopets.com/
AskTheExperts.html**–veterinary
questions answered on-line.

Breed Information

www.bestdogs.com/news/–newsgroup

**www.cheta.net/connect/canine/
breeds/**–Canine Connections Breed
Information Index

Abdominal pain, 25
Allergies
    food, 36
    humans to dogs, 2
American Kennel Club (AKC),
    55, 88
American Maltese Association, 87
American Rare Breed
    Association, 88
Anatomy, skeletal system, broken
    bones, 2, 25
Appetite, loss of, 28
Ascarids (roundworms), 28–29
Association of Pet Dog Trainers,
    88

Bald/hot spots, 29
Barking, 74
Bathing, 43–45
Bedding, crate, 6–8
Belgian Greyhound comb, 40
Bitter Apple, 11
Bleeding, 24–25
Blow drying the coat, 45
Body, 54–55
Books, 86–87
Bones, broken, 2, 25
Bowls, 8–9
Breath, stinky, 29
Breeding
    appearance, 53
    body, 54–55
    classifications, 59
    coat, 55–56
    feet, 55
    gait, 57
    head, 53–54
    legs, 55
    neck, 54
    size and weight, 56–57
    standards, 52, 54
    tail, 55
Brown dog tick, 24
Brushing
    conditioner, 40
    "flipping the wrists," 41

mats, removing, 42–43
    parting, 42
Burns, 25

Canadian Kennel Club, 88
"Canine cough" (kennel cough),
    24, 28
Cardiac-syndrome parvovirus,
    21–22
Characteristics. See Personality
Checkups, routine, 20
Chewing
    discouraging, 10–11, 74–76
    toys, 9–10, 70
Cheyletiella mange, 31
Children, 2
Classifications of breeds, 59
Coat
    bathing, 43–45
    brushing, 40
    color, 55–56
    grooming, 2, 39–40
    hot/bald spots, 29
    leisure trims, 48–49
    mats, removing, 42–43
    parting, 42
    shedding, 2
    tear staining, 47–48
    texture, 53, 55–56
    topknots, 49–51
    yellow stains, 48
Collapsing trachea, 17
Collars, 7–8, 69
Combs, 39–40
Come and sit command,
    76–78
Confinement
    babygates, 11
    during training, 71–72, 74
Coronavirus, 22
Coughing, kennel, 24
Crate
    bedding, 6–8
    feeding, 36
    location in home, 6, 11–12
    potty training, 71–72

size, 6
    traveling, 3–4

Deer tick, 24
Dehydration, 25
Delta Society, 89
Demodectic mange, 31
DHLPP vaccine, 22
Diarrhea, 21, 28
Distemper, 22–23
Dog Writers Association of
    America, 89
Down command, 78–80
Dry dog food, 33–34

Ears
    grooming, 46–47
    stinky, 29
Emergencies. See First aid
Energy, loss of, 28
External parasites, 31

Feet
    grooming, 45, 48
    shape, 55
First aid. See also Health care
    appetite, loss of, 28
    bleeding, 24–25
    coughing, 28
    diarrhea, 28
    emergencies, 25
    energy, loss of, 28
    heatstroke, 25, 27
    insect bites/stings, 27
    limping, 29
    poisonous substances, 11,
        26–27
    runny nose, 28
    shock, 25
Fits, 25
Fleas, 31
"Flipping the wrists," 41
Following while walking, 84
Food
    allergies, 36
    bowls, 8

crates, 36
  dry, 33–34
  free-feeding, 38
  growth stages, 33
  life-stage feeding, 33–34
  loss of appetite, 28
  monitoring intake, 36
  obesity, 37
  puppies, 13, 32–33
  quantity, 37–38
  reading labels, 34
  requirements, 20, 33, 36
  schedule, 12, 34–38
  table scraps, 36
Free-feeding, 38

Gait, 57
Genetic disorders
  collapsing trachea, 17
  luxated patella, 16–17
  portosystemic shunt, 15–16
  white dog shaker syndrome, 17
Grooming
  bathing, 43–45
  brushing
    conditioner, 40
    "flipping the wrists," 41
    mats, removing, 42–43
  coat, 2
  ears, 29, 46–47
  feet, 45, 48
  groomers, selecting, 51
  leisure trims, 48–49
  nails, 46
  parting, 4
  supplies, 8, 39–40
  tear staining, 47–48
  teeth, 29, 46
  topknots, 49–51
  training for, 40
  yellow stains, 48
Growth-stage feeding, 33

Halos, 54
Head

shaking, 29
shape, 53–54
Health care. *See also* First aid
  coronavirus, 22
  distemper, 22–23
  fleas, 31
  genetic disorders
    collapsing trachea, 17
    luxated patella, 16–17
    portosystemic shunt, 15–16
    white dog shaker syndrome, 17
  heartworms, 31
  hepatitis, 23
  hookworms, 30
  kennel coughing, 24
  lice, 31
  Lyme disease, 24
  mites, 31
  neutering, 18–19
  parvovirus, 21–22
  preventive, 18–20
  rabies, 20–21
  roundworms (ascarids), 28–29
  spaying, 18–19
  tapeworms, 30
  ticks, 24, 31
  vaccinations, 19, 22
  whipworms, 31
Health certificate, 3
Heartworms, 31
Heatstroke, 25, 27
Heel command, 83
Hepatitis, 23
History of breed, 58–60
Hookworms, 30
Hot/bald spots, 29
Housetraining
  crates, 6
  importance, 70
  location, 72–73
  mistakes, 71–72
  motivation, 73–74
  potty training, 71

Identification
  microchip, 12
  tags, 8, 12, 69
  tattoos, 12
Insect bites/stings, 27
Intelligence, 1
Internal parasites, 27
  heartworms, 31
  hookworms, 30
  roundworms, 28–29
  tapeworms, 30
  whipworms, 30
Itching, 29

Kennel cough ("canine cough"), 24, 28
Kong toys, 74–75

Lameness/limping 24, 29
Leashes, 7–8, 69
Legs, 55
Leisure trims, 48–49
Lice, 31
Life-stage feeding, 33–34
Lumps, 29
Lure-reward training, 66–68, 70
Luxated patella ("slipped stifles"), 16–17
Lyme disease, 24

Magazines, 87
Mange, 31
Mats in coat, removing, 42–43
Microchip (identification), 12
Milk, 13
Mites, 31

Nails, clipping, 40, 46
National Association for Search and Rescue (NASAR), 89
National Breed Club, 87
Neck, 54
Neglect of training, 63–64
Neutering, 18–19
Nose, runny, 28
Nutrition. *See* Food

Obesity, 37
Off command, 81
Origin of breed, 58–60
Orthopedic Foundation for
  Animals (OFA), 88
Oster clippers, 48–49
Owners, training, 64–65

Paralysis, 25
Parasites
  external, 31
  internal, 27–31
Parting the coat, 42
Parvovirus, 21–22
Patellar luxation, 16–17
Personality
  characteristics, 3
  with children, 2
  intelligence, 1
  socialization, 2–3, 13–14,
    65
  temperament, 57
  well-being, 20
Pin brush, 39
Play training, 67–68, 73
Poisonous substances, 11, 26–27
Popularity, 61–62
Portosystemic shunt, 15–16
Potty training, 70–74
Preventive health care, 18–20
Protein requirements, 33, 36
Punishment, 68–69
Puppies
  feeding schedule, 32–33
  proofing your home, 10–11

Rabies, 20–21
Relevancy training, 81–82
Retching/vomiting, 28
Rollover-stay command, 79–81
Roundworms (ascarids), 28–29
Routine
  establishing, 12–13
  veterinarian checkups, 20
Runny nose, 28

Sarcoptic mange, 31
Shampoos, 44–45
Shedding, 2
Shock, 25
Sit command, 77–79
Size, 56–57
Skeletal system, broken bones, 2,
  25
Slicker brush, 39
"Slipped stifles" (luxated patella),
  16–17
Socialization, 2–3, 13–14, 65
Spaying, 18–19
Stand command, 79–80
Standards for breeding. See
  Breeding
Stay command, 79–81

Table scraps, 36
Tags (identification), 8, 12
Tail, 55
Tapeworms, 30
Tattoos (identification), 12
Tear staining, 8, 47–48
Teeth
  cleaning, 46
  stinky breath, 29
Temperament, 57
Therapy Dogs International, 89
Ticks, 24, 31
Topknots, 49–51
Toys, 8, 74
  chewing, 9–10
  lure rewards, 66–68, 70
Trachea, collapsing, 17
Training
  barking, 74
  chewing, 10–11, 74–76
  classes, 64–65
  come and sit command,
    76–78
  communication, 65
  crates, 6
  following while walking, 84
  heel command, 83

house training
  location, 72–73
  mistakes, 71–72
  potty training, 71
importance of, 70
lure-reward, 66–68
motivation, 65, 73–74
neglect of, 63–64
off command, 81
owners, 64–65
play training, 67–68, 73
punishment, 68–69
relevancy, 81–82
schedules, 12–13
sit, down, stand and rollover
  command, 78–81
supplies, 69–70
trainers, 83, 88
tricks, 85
Traveling, 3–4, 6
Treats, 74–76
Tremors, 17
Tricks, 85

Unconsciousness, 25
United Kennel Club, 88

Vaccinations, 3, 19, 22
Veterinarians, 12, 20, 25
Vomiting/retching, 28

Walking
  after elimination, 73–74
  following, 84
  heel command, 83
Watchdogs, 1
Water, 8–9
Web sites, 89
Weight, 56–57
Well-being, 20
Whipworms, 30
White dog shaker syndrome, 17
Wood tick, 24

Yellow stains, 48

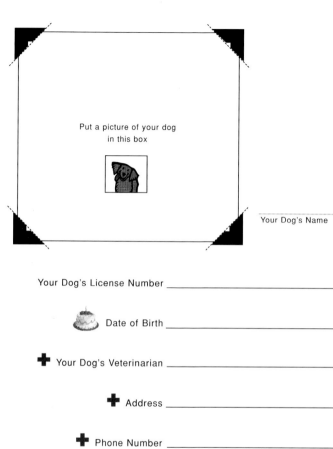

Put a picture of your dog
in this box

Your Dog's Name ....

Your Dog's License Number _____

Date of Birth _____

Your Dog's Veterinarian _____

Address _____

Phone Number _____

Medications _____

Vet Emergency Number _____

Additional Emergency Numbers _____

Feeding Instructions _____

Exercise Routine _____

Favorite Treats _____

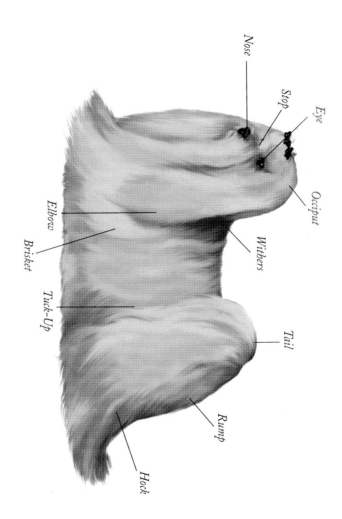

Nose

Stop

Eye

Occiput

Withers

Tail

Rump

Hock

Tuck-Up

Brisket

Elbow